THIS BOOK BELONGS TO

THE BIG LITTLE BOOK *of* AWESOME STUFF

LET'S START WITH A SECRET!

Use the decoder key on page 141 to unlock this message.
(Then use the decoder key to create your own!)

POPULAR MECHANICS

THE BIG Little BOOK of AWESOME STUFF

300 WILD FACTS, FUN PROJECTS & AMAZING TRICKS

BY DAN BOVA

TABLE OF CONTENTS

WARNING:

By opening this book, you will never be bored again. After you read the exciting pages that follow, you will actually lose the ability to yawn. We're serious.

Okay, we're not serious. It would be physically impossible to stop someone from yawning. And what's so bad about yawning anyway? Yawning puppies are, like, the cutest things ever, right?

Sorry, where were we? Oh, right. This book not being boring. That part is 100 percent true!

This super-cool handbook filled with fun projects, wildly weird facts and helpful how-tos is sure to entertain you no matter what you're into. Love running around and exploring outside? You're in luck! There's a whole chapter devoted to outdoor adventure. Are you really into art projects? Good news, there's a whole chapter on that, too! Enjoy staring at walls for hours and hours watching paint dry? Uh, sorry, you're going to have to buy a different book. We don't cover that at all.

The following pages will fill your head with wacky knowledge, like how to safely enter a black hole (page 136) and which mythological monster you definitely don't want to invite to your next pool party (page 22). Plus, we've talked to experts who will teach you how to do everything from shooting a basketball (page 98) to performing magic tricks (page 52) to writing a story that scares the pants off everyone (page 90). Don't worry, it is impossible to get nightmares from your own story.

You're also going to learn how to build some super-cool stuff! For years and years, the editors of *Popular Mechanics* have shared amazing project ideas, and we've compiled the best of the best for creative kids like you, including a floating ping-pong table (page 42), a bicycle pump-powered rocket (page 126) and a science project you can eat (page 140)!

A lot of this stuff you can do on your own, and some of the bigger projects will require help from adults. But no matter what you do, everything in here is certified 100 percent fun. And while we give you step-by-step directions, the best part is that you can adapt and modify each project to make it your own. Swap materials, change sizes, try different designs — there are no rules when it comes to the *The Big Little Book of Awesome Stuff!* (Well, except that "no being bored" one we started with.)

PROJECT DIFFICULTY LEVELS

These handy-dandy hand symbols will let you know how simple or complicated each project is. High-five!

EASY-PEASY

GET SOME HELP

ADULT NEEDED

**READY TO LEARN,
CREATE STUFF,
AND HAVE A TON OF FUN?**

WILD ADVENTURE!

"GET OUTTA HERE!"

Usually, that's a pretty rude thing to tell someone, but we're being nice in this case. Because in the following chapter, you will discover amazing facts, cool projects, and totally weird creatures that are best seen and enjoyed in the great outdoors. We've got something fun for every season, so whether it is sunny or snowing outside, good times are guaranteed!*

***LEGAL NOTE** *This guarantee does not apply if it is raining. No one has a good time in soggy socks.*

Terms You Should Know

- **HEMISPHERE** The top or bottom half of the earth, divided by the equator. (p. 20)
- **GRAVITY** The force that pulls things toward the center of Earth. (p. 11)
- **PROTRACTOR** A plastic tool that is a half-circle and used to measure angles. (p. 21)
- **MICROBES** Teeny tiny living things that can be the size of a single cell. (p. 10)
- **HYPOTHERMIA** A medical emergency where a person's body loses heat faster than it can produce heat. (p. 16)
- **GPS** The Global Positioning System, which uses satellites to determine your exact location. (p. 16)
- **LATITUDE** A coordinate that pinpoints where you are on the globe, north or south of the equator. (p. 21)

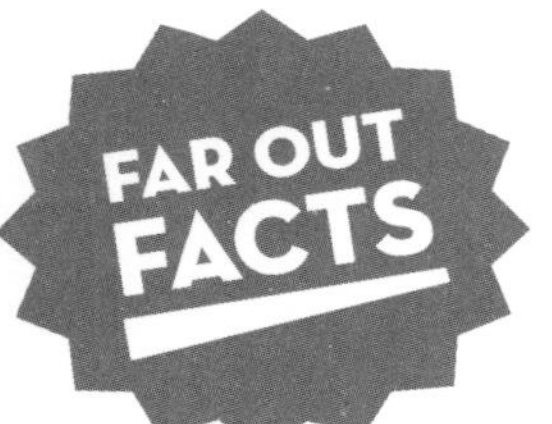

OUT-OF-THIS-WORLD THINGS TO KNOW ABOUT EARTH

A user's guide to your home planet!

1 Don't dig that hole in the sand too deep — the temperature of the Earth's core is nearly 10,000 degrees. That's the same temperature as the surface of the sun!

2 While we won't likely be visiting it anytime soon, the distance to the center of the Earth is actually pretty drivable. It's only 1,864 miles, which is like cruising from New York to Colorado (only with no rest stops).

3 If every cloud in the sky rained at once, all of the land on Earth would get covered in water. But don't worry, you won't need a boat — the layer would be the thickness of a single strand of human hair.

4 The Earth is 4.5 billion years old. People (Homo sapiens) have been around for about 450,000 years. So, if the life of Earth were a two-hour-long movie, we humans would be in it for .72 seconds. Blink and you might miss us.

5 Wondering who named Earth "Earth?" Good question — historians have no clue!

6 Earthquakes are measured in magnitude. The biggest on record was a 9.5. Scientists say that a magnitude of 12 would split the Earth in half!

7 The number of microbes living in a teaspoon of soil is equal to the number of humans currently living in Africa (1 billion!).

8 Earth isn't exactly round. It is technically an "oblate spheroid," which is like a smushed ball that is sort of flat on top and bottom and bulging in the middle. Lay off the snacks, Earth.

9 The moon's gravitation affects ocean tides — and also the length of days. Earth's rotation is slowed down by the tides, which makes days longer over time. Does that mean that school will be 14 hours in the near future? Nah. NASA says this tidal effect only adds 1.7 milliseconds every century.

10 The Earth's continents ride on giant tectonic plates that are constantly in motion. Hundreds of millions of years ago, all seven continents were smashed together to form a supercontinent called Pangaea, surrounded by one worldwide ocean. (And one really big beach!)

11 Trees should get more birthday presents than any living thing on earth. Lots of them live for more than 100 years, but the oldest tree on record was a Great Basin Bristlecone Pine that scientists say was more than 5,000 years old!

12 It is hard to get lost when you stand at the North Pole — every direction you turn is South.

13 Deserts are places that have less than 10 inches of rain or snow per year. And they don't have to be hot! Antarctica is actually the largest desert on the planet.

14 Since rivers don't have perfect start and endpoints, scientists debate whether the Nile or the Amazon is the longest river. But the Amazon is definitely the world's largest river by volume and holds about 20 percent of all the freshwater on Earth!

15 Ninety-four percent of living creatures call the ocean their home, including the Blue Whale, the biggest on the planet. They weigh 400,000 pounds, which is about the same as 33 elephants!

HOW TO IDENTIFY ANIMAL TRACKS

Next time you're hiking, look down to see who trotted by before you.

DOG

Pooch paw prints have an oval shape (as opposed to a more circular one from cats) and have a triangular hind mark with four toes and distinct claw marks.

TURKEY

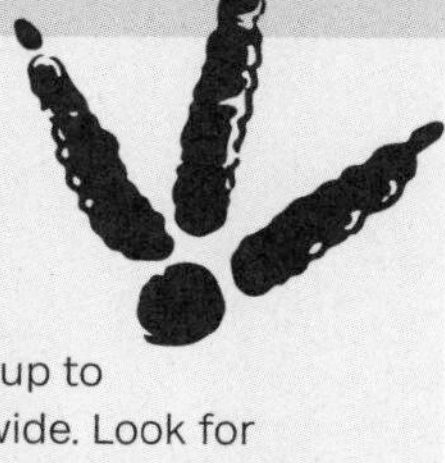

These are easy to spot as they can be up to five inches wide. Look for three long front toe marks. (And a side of stuffing if it is Thanksgiving season.)

DEER

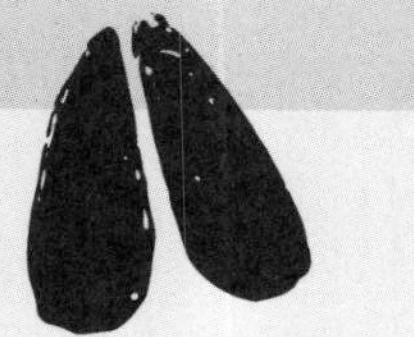

This drawing shows a walking deer. A running deer will spread its toes, and the print will look more like a V.

BLACK BEAR

Smaller than a grizzly bear, but just as scary! If you see a bear in front of you, calmly walk backward in the other direction, keeping an eye on your furry friend.

SKUNK

A skunk's hind feet leave prints that look like a human's (but are, like, 10,000 times more smelly!).

TRAIN

They might look cute, but our expert advice: Never try to pet a train.

DON'T SMELL THESE ROSES!

Plants you definitely want to avoid in the woods.

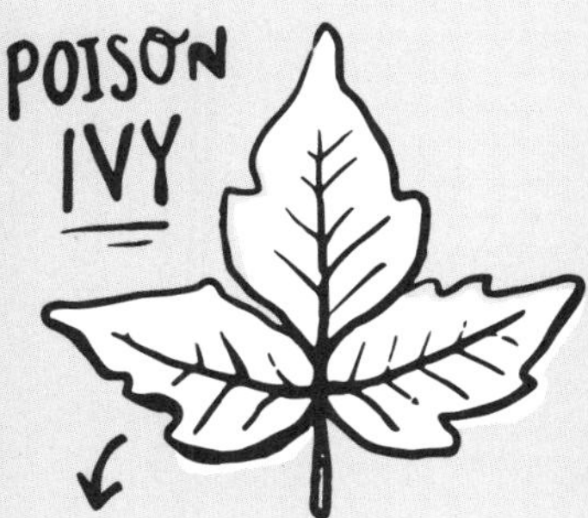

POISON IVY

LOOKS LIKE
There's a saying, "Leaves of three, let it be." Poison ivy grows in leaf clutters of three, and the leaflet in the middle usually has a longer stem. The leaves can be green or red, and either shiny or dull. Tricky!

WHY TO AVOID IT
Causes super-itchy skin rashes and blisters.

POISON HEMLOCK

LOOKS LIKE
Poison hemlock stems can grow very high, are hollow and typically have purplish-red splotching or streaks on them. The flowers are white and come in round clusters; each flower has five petals.

WHY TO AVOID IT
Eating it is extremely hazardous and can cause death. Don't eat!

POISON SUMAC

LOOKS LIKE
Poison sumac has leaves made up of five to 13 smooth-edged leaflets (always an odd number). They have red stems, and in spring, summer and fall, they have clusters of small berries.

WHY TO AVOID IT
Has the same effects as poison ivy, only worse. (Yes, that is possible.)

DID YOU KNOW? People can get a poison ivy rash, but your pets can't. (Lucky dogs!)

GIMME SHELTER

Build yourself a cool place to hang out whether it is warm or freezing outside.

HOW TO Build a Teepee

DIFFICULTY LEVEL

STUFF YOU'LL NEED

- **Nine poles** (Depending on how big you want it, 6' to 10' long will work)
- **Some rope**
- **12' x 15' canvas drop cloth** (or an old bed sheet)

DID YOU KNOW?

Teepees were used by Native American tribes like the Apaches and Comanches because they were easy to pickup and move while following migrating herds of buffalo on the Great Plains.

1 **BUILD A TRIPOD**
Put three poles together, and wrap the rope around them about 18 inches from one end. Tie off snugly.

2 **FILL IN SUPPORT POLES**
Stand up the three poles and spread them out so they stand like a tripod, then lay the six remaining poles in the gaps.

3 **COVER IT UP**
Drape the canvas cloth over the frame. (You might need a chair or ladder.) Tie the corners for a tight fit up top.

4 **TRIM TO FIT**
Use scissors to cut off the excess canvas at the bottom.

5 **MOVE IN!**
Add a blanket for the floor and any comfy pillows and you're good to go!

HOW TO Build an Igloo

DIFFICULTY LEVEL

STUFF YOU'LL NEED

- **Lots of snow!**
- **Snow shovel**
- **Saw** (or something you can use to cut snow blocks)
- **A stick**
- **6' to 10' of string**
- **A shoebox**

1 **CREATE BUILDING BLOCKS (TWO WAYS!)**

- *Option One:* Use the shovel to dig a long trench in packed down snow and the saw to cut blocks (12 inches wide, 24 inches long and 18 inches deep).
- *Option Two:* Use the shoe box as a mold to make your blocks.

2 **CIRCLE UP**

Mark the center of where the igloo will stand with a stick. Tie the string and use it to trace a circle.

3 **START TO STACK**

Lay the first level of blocks along the circle. Use the saw to cut in a ramp up that extends halfway around the row.

4 **LEVEL UP**

Lay on the next layers, going up the ramp so that the blocks are coiling upward. Cut a slight incline into the top of each brick.

5 **GET SMALLER**

Keep layering up, using slightly smaller blocks as you go up until you have a roof.

6 **PACK IT IN**

Shovel snow onto the outer walls to fill in any gaps.

7 **TIME TO CHILL!**

Carve in a front door and some side holes for ventilation. Time to chill in your new snow home!

REAL LIFE ADVENTURE

MAROONED IN THE ARCTIC (WITH POLAR BEARS!)

The incredible survival story of a helicopter pilot who crashed in the icy waters of the Arctic Circle.

IN 2015, RUSSIAN ADVENTURER SERGEY ANANOV tried to become the first person to circle the globe in a personal helicopter — and he wound up having a lot more excitement than he bargained for.

While flying over the Davis Strait, a frigid finger of ocean separating Canada and Greenland, his trusty Robinson R22 helicopter had a severe engine malfunction and started to fall out of the sky like a rock.

The expert pilot tried to land the plummeting aircraft on an ice floe that was about the size of a basketball court, but soon realized it was too far away to reach. So, he glided the helicopter into the water, tilting it to the side so the whirling blades would hit the waves and smash off, making it safer for him to escape.

Sergey had to think fast. He was wearing a thick survival suit designed to keep people alive if they fall in freezing water, but it wasn't zipped up all the way and water was flooding in.

As the helicopter sunk into the murky water, he had time only to grab one thing. His choices were a satellite phone, a distress beacon, a GPS tracker, or a life raft. All were super-valuable, but he realized that if he couldn't float in this water, he was doomed. So, he went for the life raft. Problem: it was stuck under his seat! He tried and tried to pull it out with no luck. With moments to spare, he swam out of the helicopter door to the surface, took a deep breath, then plunged back into the black, salty water, slipped into the sinking helicopter, and finally freed the raft.

Sergey paddled himself over to the ice floe and pulled himself up. He was terrified but made himself calm down and think. His next few decisions could mean life or death. First, he took off his soaked survival suit, emptied and wrung it out the best he could, then climbed back in before hypothermia hit. He flipped over the raft and laid under it, using it as a kind of tent to protect him from the high winds. To make sure it didn't blow away, he tied it to his foot.

Things were bad, but they were about to get worse. A few hours later, Sergey realized that he was not alone on the ice floe. From underneath the raft, he heard heavy breathing and crunching snow. Peeking out, he saw what he feared — a monster-sized polar bear! He was beyond scared and knew there was no way he could win a fight with this visitor. So, with no other options, Sergey went wild. He jumped up and ran straight at the polar bear, yelling and waving his arms, with the raft that was tied to his foot bouncing behind him. It worked! The bear was confused and wandered off, leaving Sergey alone again.

But he wouldn't be alone for long. Over the course of the next few hours, he was visited by a total of three bears, all of which he was able to scare off in the same way. He knew his luck wouldn't last for long, and he also knew that he will soon get dehydrated. (One of the most terrible parts of being stranded at sea is being surrounded by water that you cannot drink — salt water will only speed up your demise.) It was hard to stay hopeful.

What Sergey didn't know, however, was that his friend, Andrey Kaplan, was back home tracking his journey online. And he noticed that the GPS signal from Sergey's helicopter went dead. Leaping into action, he made some phone calls and soon a rescue squad from Halifax, Nova Scotia was on the hunt for the lost adventurer.

Sergey had some signal flares in his raft supplies, but unfortunately, there was incredibly thick fog in the area and the flares had little chance of being seen. He could hear planes and helicopters, but they had no chance of seeing him or his signals. Then, miraculously, with just one hour of daylight left, the fog lifted and rescuers saw the final glint of light from Sergey's last flare. A helicopter flew to the ice floe where one more time Sergey was running around, screaming his head off and wildly flapping his arms. Luckily, this time he wasn't doing it to scare away bears — it was out of joy. Thirty-six hours after being marooned on a slab of ice, he was rescued!

THINGS YOU DIDN'T KNOW ABOUT POLAR BEARS

FURRY FACTS FROM THE WWF

- **Their fur is actually clear, but the sun's reflection makes it looks white.**
- **Underneath that fur, they have thick black skin and layers of blubber that help keep them warm.**
- **They typically weigh between 800 and 1,330 pounds.**
- **Polar bears spend 50 percent of their day looking for food.**
- **They can smell seals hiding under three feet of snow.**

- **They can swim 6 MPH.**
- **You won't see them on the South Pole looking for penguin snacks — wild polar bears live only in the north.**

HERE COME THE WATERWORKS!

Two wet ways to beat the heat.

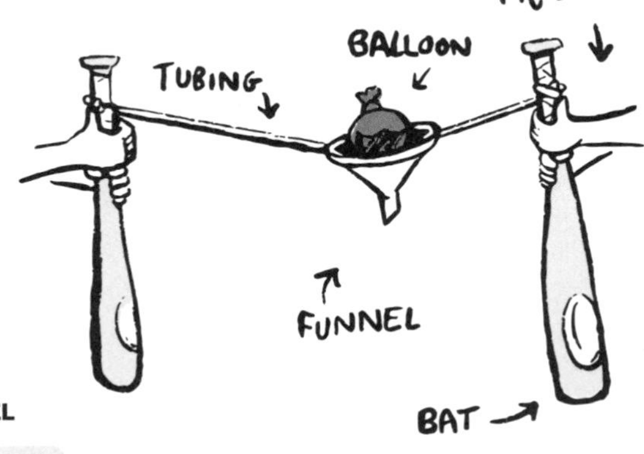

Water Balloon Launcher — Attack!

DIFFICULTY LEVEL

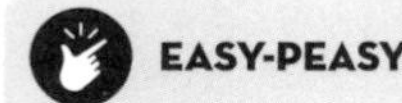

Your next water balloon fight is going to be epic.

STUFF YOU'LL NEED

- 2 strong friends
- 2 baseball bats or lacrosse sticks
- 1 plastic funnel, 6" diameter
- 4' of surgical tubing
- Lots of balloons

1 **DRILL**
Cut hole on opposites sides of the funnel, about one inch from the lip.

2 **SNIP AND TIE**
Cut the surgical tubing in half. Tie one end through a funnel hole and the other end to a bat. Do the same on the other hole.

3 **READY, AIM, FIRE!**
Have your helpers hold each bat upright, pull back the funnel, load in a water balloon and drench your enemies!

Drive-Thru Bike Wash

Clean your ride and cool down at the same time!

DIFFICULTY LEVEL

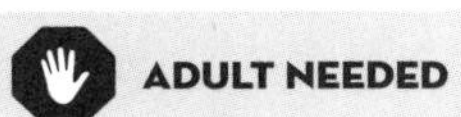

STUFF YOU'LL NEED

- **22 ½' of ¾" PVC**
- **One ¾" screw-on hose connector**
- **Two PVC tee connectors**
- **Two 90-degree elbows**
- **Three end caps**
- **PVC cement**
- **Hacksaw**
- **Drill**

You can order all of this online from any major home improvement store.

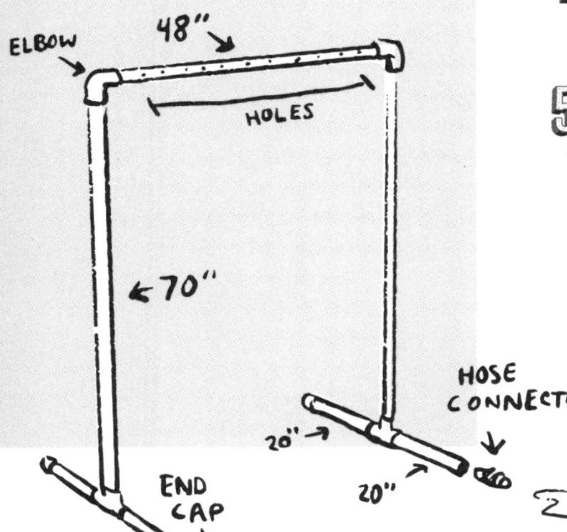

1 **MAKE THE FEET**
Connect two 20-inch pieces of PVC with a tee. One foot should be closed off with two end caps. The other needs an end cap on one side and a hose connector on the other (to connect the hose from the house).

2 **START THE TOP**
Insert 70-inch pieces of PVC in the open ends of the tees and place a 90-degree elbow on the ends.

3 **DRILL TIME**
Take a 48-inch piece of PVC and drill ¼-inch holes evenly spaced across, about one every two inches.

4 **ATTACH THE TOP**
Place the drilled piece (with holes down) into the ends of the elbows. At this point, you'll have what looks like a doorway.

5 **LET 'ER RIP!**
If it all fits properly, glue each connection with the PVC cement following direction on the packaging. Once fully dry, connect a garden hose, turn on the valve and you're open for business!

LOOK UP!

SPOT THE COOL CONSTELLATIONS

How to connect the dots in the sky.

A constellation is a group of stars whose shape looks like something — an animal, an object, or sometimes an ancient god. There are 88 official constellations, and these five are some of the easier ones to spot in the northern hemisphere sky. Can you find them?

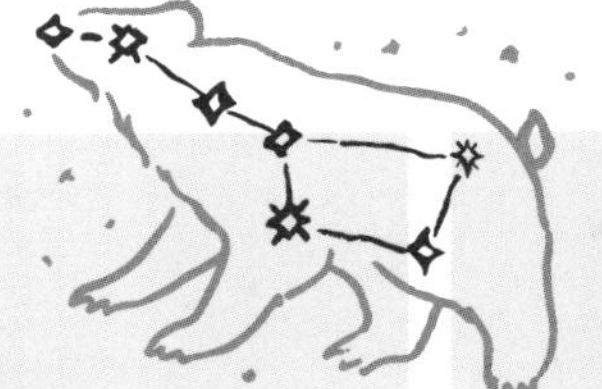

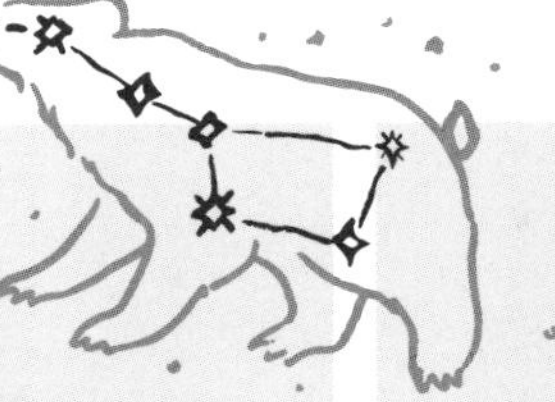

URSA MAJOR

The Great Bear

Look north above the horizon for the Big Dipper, a pattern that resembles a kitchen ladle. The handle of the Big Dipper makes up Ursa Major's head (or tail, whichever way you imagine the bear facing!)

URSA MINOR

The Little Bear

If you spotted the Big Dipper, the two outer stars of its bowl point right to the North Star, which is the end of the Dipper Jr.'s handle.

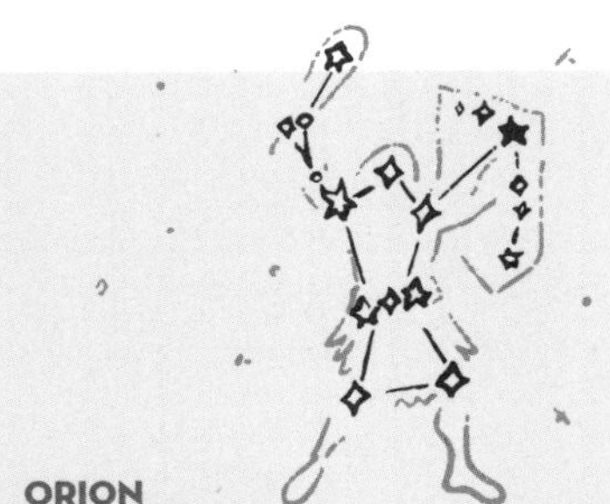

ORION

The Hunter

To find Orion, look for his belt, which is formed by three stars that form a line across his waist.

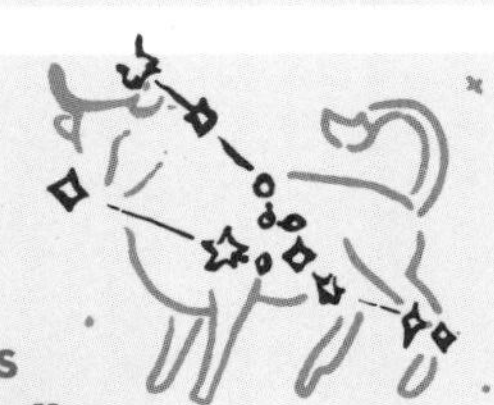

TAURUS

The Bull

This bull is easy to find because one of the main stars, Aldebaran, is helpfully one of the brightest in the night sky. And Orion's belt points right at it to the northeast!

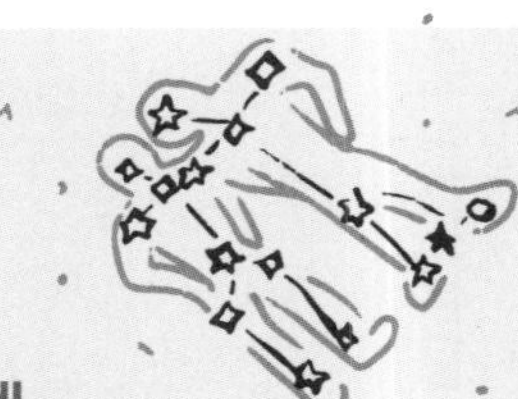

GEMINI

The Twins

Above and to the left of Orion, this constellation's two brightest stars, Castor and Pollux, represent the heads of the twin brothers.

Find Your Latitude with the Sky!

DIFFICULTY LEVEL

Build a simple version of a tool called a sextant that explorers have used throughout history to find out where in the world they are!

STUFF YOU'LL NEED

- A straw
- A protractor
- String
- Washer (or Life Savers candy)
- Tape

1 **TAPE IT UP**
Tape the straw to the straight part of the protractor.

2 **TIE TIME**
Tie one end of the string to the center hole on the protractor and the other end to the washer or candy.

3 **TAKE A LOOK**
Find the North Star (it is the last star on the handle of the Little Dipper) and look at it through the straw. Have a friend write down the angle number on the protractor that the string lines up with. Subtract that number from 90 and that's your latitude. Check your math out by using a globe. Are you where you think you are?

NORTH STAR

A FIELD GUIDE TO MYTHICAL CREATURES

Everything you need to know about Bigfoot, the Loch Ness Monster and their creepiest friends!

BIGFOOT

Origin: Unknown

Bigfoot (also known as Sasquatch) is thought to be the missing link between humans and apes. There are people who have dedicated their lives to finding Bigfoot — he even has his very own official FBI file! But sadly, Bigfoot is as shy as he is hairy. No one has been able to find proof that he actually exists.

MEDUSA

Origin: Greek

If you see Medusa, look away fast! She had the power to turn a person into stone with a single glance. If that isn't bad enough, Medusa has snakes for hair. Wonder what kind of shampoo she uses?

KRAKEN

Origin: Nordic Folklore

The mythical Kraken is a giant squid-like creature. When it gets hungry, it likes to come to the surface and eat entire ships, crew members and all. Hey Kraken, maybe try snacking on Goldfish? They're much tastier and way easier to digest than a ship anchor.

VAMPIRES

Origin: Eastern Europe

The world's most famous vampire is Dracula. A few things to know: They suck blood to live, never age, can turn into bats, and hate garlic. If you ever face one, offer it a slice of Pizza Hut and watch him dissolve.

LOCH NESS MONSTER

Origin: Nordic Scottish

The Loch Ness Monster is believed to be a dinosaur (a plesiosaur, to be exact) that managed to escape extinction by living in the deep Scottish Loch Ness Lake. The first written account of the beast appeared in 565 A.D., so after over a thousand years of swimming around, Nessie is probably very, very, very good at doing the backstroke.

SIRENS

Origin: Greek

Sirens are a mythological species that hang out on rock outcroppings by the sea and use their beautiful and enchanted singing voices to make sailors steer too close and crash. We wonder what their favorite karaoke song is.

ABOMINABLE SNOWMAN

Origin: Asian

You might know the Abominable Snowman by another name, Yeti. But no matter what you call it, all the stories tend to be the same: Somewhere in the mountains, this humanoid creature wanders around the snow. No one knows exactly why. Maybe he can't remember where he left his snowboard?

JERSEY DEVIL

Origin: American

The Jersey Devil haunts New Jersey's Pine Barrens and has reportedly been around since 1735. This creature has a horse-like head with horns and walks on its two hind legs. He'd probably be very popular at petting zoos.

MINOTAUR

Origin: Greek

The Minotaur is half-man, half-bull. In order to stop him from trying to eat people, he got locked inside a giant maze to run around in. Doesn't sound like the worst time out to us!

CHIMERA

Origin: Greek

There is *a lot* going on with the Chimera: It has a fire-breathing lion's head, a goat's body, and a serpent tail. According to Greek mythology, the Chimera's dad is a monster named Typhon, and its mom is a half-woman, half-snake named Echidna. Our suggestion: Avoid hanging out at Chimera's house after school.

DIRTY JOB: GROW AN INDOOR HERB GARDEN

DIFFICULTY LEVEL

A science project you can eat!

These three herbs are very easy to grow — and very delicious to eat. You'll need to find a spot near a window that gets at least six hours of sunlight every day to get good results. You can begin by growing seeds in an empty egg carton packed with soil, but as they start to sprout, you'll eventually need to move to them to bigger pots you can find at any gardening store. Ready to get dirty?

BASIL

GROWING TIP

Basil likes lots of sun and water — try to keep the soil moist, but not drenched. And this is weird: Pinching the top of the plant encourages it to grow. Sorry basil!

TASTES GREAT ON

English muffin pizzas

MINT

GROWING TIP

They prefer a cool, shady spot, but can also grow in the sun. They spread fast, so you'll have a bunch before you know it! And bonus, they are perennials, which means they grow back year after year.

TASTES GREAT IN

Iced tea or even plain water

CHIVES

GROWING TIP

Super-easy to grow, and they get this cool purple flower on the end that is totally edible. Wait till they're about six inches long before you start to harvest their oniony-tasting leaves. Snip low and they'll grow back!

TASTES GREAT ON

Baked potatoes and nachos

If you buy plants from a gardening center, the roots will be super-packed in a ball when you take them out of their container. Break up the root ball by squeezing it gently to loosen and separate the roots before you plant in the pots. This allows the roots to spread out into the soil to make it more stable and find more water.

MAKE A RECYCLED BOTTLE BIRD FEEDER

DIFFICULTY LEVEL

Reduce waste and fill some tweeters' tummies at the same time.

STUFF YOU'LL NEED

- An empty plastic bottle
- Sticks or pencils, about 8" to 10" long
- Metal screw hook
- String
- Birdseed

1 **CLEAN IT UP**
Clean the bottle thoroughly, removing any labels or glue.

2 **THE TOPPER**
Screw the metal hook screw into the bottle cap.

3 **MAKE PERCHES**
Poke very small holes about two inches from the bottom on opposite sides of the bottle. Push a stick or pencil through it. It should fit snugly. This will be a bird perch. Move up two or three inches and make another set of holes on the other side of the bottle. Repeat depending on how big your bottle allows. Stop when you're about three inches from the cap.

4 **DINNER DOORS**
About one to two inches above each perch, use a knife to cut a small ⅛-inch opening. These will be little windows for the birds to get the grub. (Don't make them too big or else the bird seed will pour out.)

5 **CHOW TIME**
Fill with birdseed. If the windows are too big, you can use a little tape to narrow the gaps.

AWESOME (AND EASY) PET TRICKS!

Whether you have a new puppy or an older dog, here are a few simple tricks.

TRAINER TIP

As your pooch is starting to learn, it is very important to repeat the trick's command after they do it and right before you give them the treat. This helps their doggy brain connect the words with the action that gets the yummy prize!

HIGH-FIVE

Hold a treat in your fist. Say "High-five!" while tapping one of your dog's front paws with your other hand. Your dog will likely raise the paw you are tapping to knock the treat out of your fist. Say "High-five!" again and reward with the treat.

TWIRL

Hold a treat up to your doggy's schnoz, then circle it around their head slow enough so they turn to follow it. Once you make a complete spin, repeat the command "Twirl!" and then give them the prize.

KISS

Some think this is cute, some think it is gross. But if your like dog lickies, hold a treat up to your cheek and say “Kiss!” When your dog moves in, sneak the treat away. When they make contact with your cheek, say “Kiss” and then give them the reward.

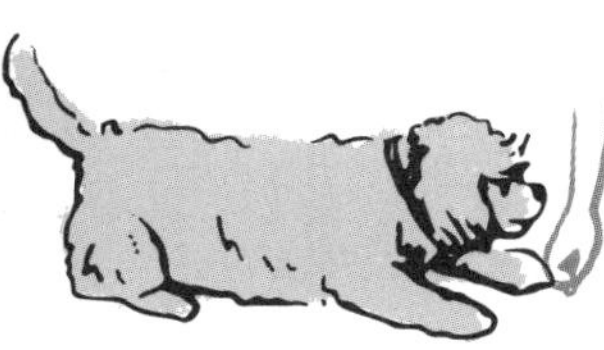

CRAWL

When your dog is in a belly-down position, hold a treat a few inches out of their reach. Slowly move it back as they scooch forward to get a nibble. Reward with a little piece every couple of inches, repeating the command “Crawl!” every time.

SLALOM

This is a more involved trick but a ton of fun. Set up a few evenly spaced flexible poles that you can buy from a pet store. (You can use soccer cones if you have them.) Hold a treat in your hand and lead your athlete zigging in and out of the course. Reward at the end and, as always, repeat the command. As your superstar catches on, add more poles or cones to make it a challenge.

NO TOWEL? NO PROBLEM!

THE SCIENCE OF HOW DOGS SHAKE THEMSELVES DRY

With just a few shakes, wet dogs can remove about 70 percent of the water from their fur!

How fast a dog must shake to become dry depends on the radius of its tummy. The bigger their abdomen, the lower the frequency at which the pooch has to shake. That means that a labrador retriever doesn't have to shake nearly as quickly as a soggy chihuahua.

Dogs rotate their spines about 30 degrees with each twist. But their loose skin continues to move way past that. In fact, their skin can go a total of 100 degrees in either direction.

Scientists have studied dogs' shaking abilities and used what they learned to make better clothes washing machines. Wait. Dogs help keep things clean?!

INCREDIBLE
BUILDS
CHAPTER
2
TWO

How can you tell if a carpenter is nervous?
They bite their nails.

Okay, that was terrible, but don't worry, we won't make any more bad woodworking puns — we wouldn't want to *screw* up this introduction. Okay, okay, now we're really done. In the following pages, you will find plans for super-cool builds and learn about some of the most amazing things ever created. See? We said no more construction puns and we kept our promise. Why wood you doubt us?

Terms You Should Know

- **"** Symbol used for inches in measurements. (p. 40)
- **BIPEDAL** An animal that uses two legs for walking. (p. 38)
- **CROSSCUT** Cutting across the wood grain. (p. 36)
- **PHYSICS** The science of motion. (p. 38)
- **PVC** A type of plastic that usually comes as white pipes. (p. 34)
- **RAFTER SQUARE** A tool that is shaped like a triangle that can be used for many things, like marking a right angle. (p. 36)
- **SCALING LAWS** A relationship between two objects that make them get bigger or smaller. (p. 38)
- **SUSTAINABLE** A way of doing things that supports the environment and human health. (p. 30)
- **WHOOPS** A common expression said when you cut something before double-checking that your measurements are correct.

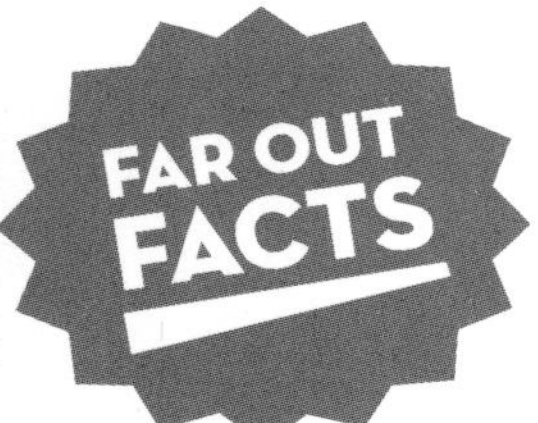

MIND-BLOWING FACTS ABOUT BUILDING

12 fascinating tidbits about tools, materials and the most amazing things ever made.

1 The first tools invented by humans were sharpened stones used for cutting, chopping, and scraping. The oldest remains of a tool were found in Africa — made 2.6 million years ago!

2 The largest log cabin in the world is called Granot Loma — it has 27 fireplaces, 23 bedrooms and 13 bathrooms. People who live there must have to pee a lot.

3 Balsa wood is one of the lightest on earth. That makes it great for building model airplanes. (And terrible at surviving encounters with curious pets.)

4 The opposite of balsa is ebony, a kind of hardwood that is so dense that it sinks in water. Note: Don't make your canoe out of ebony.

5 The world's biggest construction project is the Great Wall of China. It is 13,170.7 miles long and, in some spots, is 40 feet tall. How annoying would it be if you accidentally kicked a ball over it?

6 Bamboo is a great building material for two reasons: It is the fastest growing land plant in the world (It has been recorded growing three feet in just 24 hours.) which makes it super-sustainable. And it's also incredibly strong — even stronger than steel!

10 Timber is a tree grown specifically to provide wood for carpentry and construction. If you hear someone yell, "Timber!" look out — that's what lumberjacks shout right before they cut down a tree!

11 Humans aren't the only ones who use tools: Chimpanzees make spear-like weapons for hunting, and sea otters use rocks to crack open shellfish. Sure hope they wear safety glasses.

12 Talk about an out-of-this-world project: The International Space Station was put together in space piece by piece. It took 18 launches between 1998 and 2011 to get everything up there. You definitely want to check twice that you have everything before you go up—the nearest hardware store is 250 miles away on Earth.

7 How's this for a house? In the 13th Century, Italian explorer Marco Polo described the amazing palace of Kublai Khan in the Mongol empire: It was covered with gold and silver and had a dining room big enough to seat 6,000 people. And here's the unbelievable part: The palace was built out of bamboo sections that could be taken apart and reassembled wherever Khan wanted to go.

8 In the 1800s, German company C&E Fein invented the first power tool: a combination of an electric motor and a hand drill. Hole-y cow, that makes drilling easier!

9 One of the most common types of lumber is the 2x4. And it's got a secret: The measurements of a 2x4 is actually 1.5 inches by 3.5 inches! It starts out at two inches by four inches, but the wood gets shaved down to create smooth edges and sometimes shrinks a bit while drying.

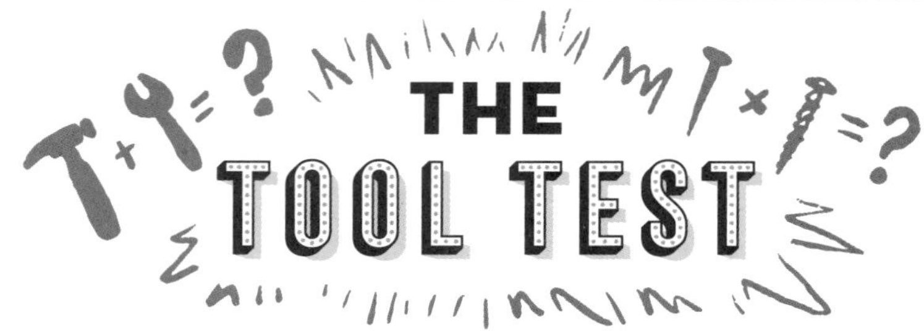

1. When using power tools (or standing near someone using them), which protective equipment should you wear?

A. Safety goggles
B. Kneepads and shin guards
C. Helmet
D. Safety goggles, gloves and ear protection

2. When using a level, how do you know your surface is straight?

A. When the level can be pressed flat against the surface
B. When the level is against the surface, and the air bubble is between the two lines
C. When the air bubble reaches the top of the tube
D. When the air bubble pops

3. What is a washer?

A. A machine that washes your dirty clothes
B. A screw with a wide flat head
C. A long tube used to connect two objects
D. A thin donut-shaped plate that sits under a bolt or screw

4. What is a stripped screw?

A. A screw that has no packaging
B. A screw with a damaged head that is difficult to turn
C. A headless screw
D. A screw that forgot to get dressed

5. If you need to tighten a bolt, which tool would you use?

A. Wrench
B. Screwdriver
C. Hammer
D. Roll of duct tape

6. What is a hammer not good for?

A. Hitting in nails
B. Gently tapping wood pieces into place
C. Yanking out bent nails
D. Flipping pancakes

ANSWER KEY | **1.** D | **2.** B | **3.** D | **4.** B | **5.** A | **6.** D

THE BASICS OF BASIC TOOLS

Quick tips for budding woodworkers.

HAMMER
Grip a hammer as if you're shaking hands with somebody. When you need more control (like if you're starting a nail into a board) hold it closer to the hammer's head. When you need power, grip the hammer near the bottom of the handle. (See pg. 35 for more hammer how-tos.)

SANDPAPER
It comes in three grades: coarse, medium, and fine. Coarse is used to take away very rough edges, medium will help takeaway imperfections like dents and fine will make things super-smooth. Wrap the paper around a small wood block and use that block to do your sanding. Always sand with the grain. Going across it will create scratches.

SCREWDRIVER
Make a small hole (with a drill or a hole punch) where you want the screw to go. Then, holding the screw and tip of the screwdriver with one hand, guide the screw tip into the hole and apply slight pressure as you turn the screwdriver. Once the screw starts to dig into the wood, you can put more muscle into it.

Make Your Own Glue

DIFFICULTY LEVEL

A simple recipe perfect for any paper project.

STUFF YOU'LL NEED

- **1 cup of flour**
- **⅓ cup of sugar**
- **1-½ cups of water**
- **1 tsp. of vinegar**

1. Add all of the ingredients into a saucepan. (Use about one cup of water to start and add as needed.)
2. Warm the mixture with medium heat, stirring until it thickens up to a nice goopy consistency.
3. Let the mixture cool and get gluing!

STICKY SUPERHERO: DUCT TAPE

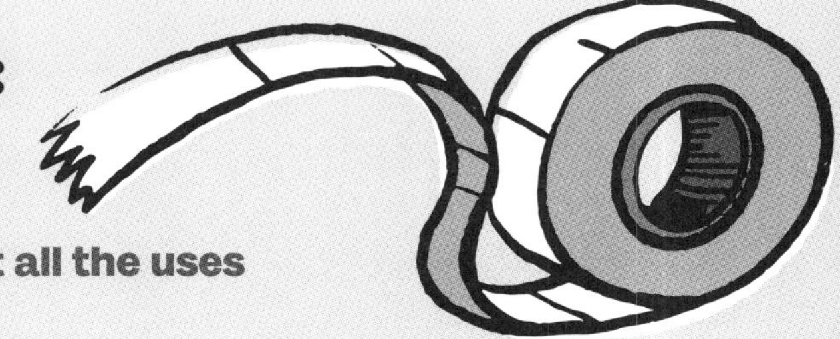

We could write an entire book about all the uses for this glorious stuff.

Super-strong and waterproof duct tape (originally called "duck tape") was invented during World War II to seal up and then quickly open ammunition boxes. Since then, people have found hundreds (maybe even thousands) of uses. Here are 10 surprising things duct tape can do:

Repair a rip in a tent ceiling. Pull the edges of the tear so that they slightly overlap. This will form a waterproof seal with one piece of tape.

Remove splinters. Place the sticky part over the splinter and peel it back.

Catch flies. Hang a length of tape off the ceiling and flies won't be able to resist tasting its sticky sweetness — or get unstuck.

Fix a hole in a toothpaste tube. Toothpaste squirting out the wrong end? A well-placed piece will seal it right up. Fix the mess and your smile!

Open a tight jar. Wrap a length around the lid and pull the end like the ripcord of a lawnmower.

Save a tree. A tree branch that has been damaged in a storm but not fully broken off can be healed over time by tightly wrapping it up like a cast.

Help with blisters. If you don't have a Band-Aid handy, place a small piece of tissue paper over your blister, then use a small piece of duct tape to hold it in place.

Make a portable dog bowl. Wrap duct tape around a bowl (sticky side out) to get the shape, then add another layer (sticky side in). You have a light, collapsible bowl.

Build a canoe. This involves using a ton of tape! But if you build a frame out of wood or PVC, it is possible to make a watertight watercraft.

Make a super Wiffle Ball bat. Wrapping a Wiffle Ball bat in duct tape will give it added weight to send home run balls flying.

How to Hammer a Nail

DIFFICULTY LEVEL

Popular Mechanics' woodworking wiz Roy Berendsohn shares hard-hitting advice.

1 **LOSE YOUR FEAR**
Lose your fear of hitting your fingers. You will. It's going to hurt. Get over it.

2 **GET IN POSITION**
If you're right-handed, place your left foot slightly in front of your right. Spread your feet shoulder-width apart. Bend your knees.

3 **GET A GRIP**
When you need to swing with more force, grip the handle as close to the end as possible. For less force, choke up on the handle. Don't use more force to drive a nail than you have to. You're trying to drive the nail, not kill it. And establish a rhythm. Rhythm is what makes the work happen.

4 **KEEP GOING**
If you bend a nail, start another one nearby and keep going. Later, go back and pull the one you bent. It's less disheartening to fix a mistake when you can look at all the work you've done well.

Make a Ball Toss Carnival Game

Step right up and try your luck!

DIFFICULTY LEVEL

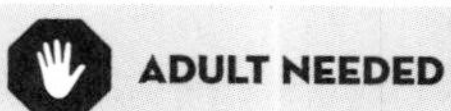

STUFF YOU'LL NEED

- **4 1" round-head wood screws**
- **1 ¼ sheet of ¼" plywood**
- **6 ¼" x 3" x 2' poplar boards**
- **1 piece of 2'x4'** (at least 30" long)
- **6 balls** (1 ½" tennis, practice golf, or Nerf-gun balls)
- **Saw**
- **Drill**
- **Hole saw bit**
- **Wood glue**
- **Tape measure**
- **Rafter square**

1. Use a table saw to rip the plywood to 16 inches wide, then crosscut it into two pieces. One piece (which will become the target board) should be 21 inches long. The other (which will be the back) should be 24 inches.

2. Cut five 24-inch-long strips from the ¼-inch poplar boards. These will become spacer-strips that separate the balls inside the ball toss. Cut the sixth poplar to 16 inches.

3. Mark the spacer-strip locations on the target board side and the backside of the ball toss using a pencil, tape measure, and rafter square. The space between each strip should be about 3 ¹¹⁄₁₆ inches, but there's no need to get fussy. As long as you mark both boards with identical spacing, everything will line up.

4 Use a drill and the hole saw to bore holes in the target board, making sure the holes are centered between the lines. Do three sizes of holes: big, medium and small. (Make sure small is still big enough to fit a ball into.) Glue the spacer strips to the target board and let the glue dry for an hour.

5 Apply a band of glue on top of each spacer strip and press the backboard into position. Place a weighted object on the board to hold it down while the glue dries.

6 Glue the 16-inch poplar board to the bottom of the spacer strips and let the glue dry for 15 minutes.

7 Cut two 15-inch-long 2x4 pieces, then cut a 56-degree angle on the end of each piece to create the legs.

8 Attach the game board to the legs with the round-head wood screws.

9 Work time is over.
Let's play!

THE RULES OF BALL TOSS

Stand four feet from the board and try to bounce a ball into the holes.

The biggest holes are worth one point. Medium holes, three. Small holes, five.

Alternate turns, first player to reach 21 wins!

WANT A 60-FOOT ROBOT TO WALK? BEND THE LAWS OF PHYSICS.

IF YOU VISIT YAMASHITA PIER IN JAPAN, you can expect to see cargo ships, tugboats — oh, and also the world's largest humanoid robot.

Modeled after the RX-782-2 Gundam fictional robot that has appeared in TV shows and manga comics, this metal monster stands nearly 60 feet tall on two feet!

We know what you're thinking: What if the big guy decides he's bored standing on the pier and decides to rampage through the nearby town? Well, anyone worried that the bipedal bot will get a mind of its own and go bonkers can relax: While Gundam can move in many directions, its designers are having some trouble getting it to walk.

The problem is its size. If you want something huge to move, you need powerful motors and a super-strong frame to keep it together. But here's where it gets tricky: All of the big motors and steel framing inside Gundam make it even heavier and therefore harder to move. This is something called scaling laws in physics, and engineers are challenged to find new technology and different uses of materials to get around the pesky rules of the universe.

So, while Gundam can't walk right now, it can give a friendly wave hello to people visiting him in Japan. And we've seen enough crazy sci-fi movies about technology that tries to wipe out humanity to know that maybe that is the best thing for all of us!

ROBOTS AT WORK

THEY'RE SUPER-HELPFUL—AND NEVER NEED A LUNCH BREAK!

BURGER FLIPPERS
Flippy the robot cooks fast-food burgers. Want fries with that? Flippy makes those too!

POLICE DOGS
Several cities are experimenting with dog-like bots that can help first responders avoid dangerous situations.

FACTORY WORKERS
Robots can build anything from washing machines to Tesla cars and can help move heavy boxes around warehouses.

CLEANERS
There's a good chance that a robot cleaned up the Cheerios you spilled this morning—more than 30 million Roomba vacuums have been sold around the world.

Totally Sweet Project

Make a candy delivery chute.

DIFFICULTY LEVEL

FUN-SIZE CANDY FACTS

- No wonder we need such big Trick or Treat bags: About 600 million pounds of candy are given out every Halloween.
- During World War II, American soldiers were given Tootsie Rolls because they provided quick bursts of energy and didn't melt or spoil in the heat.
- The world's largest lollipop would take a long time to eat — it weighed over 7,000 pounds!
- The name Snickers comes from inventor Frank Mars' favorite horse named Snickers.
- Skittles are the most popular non-chocolate candy, and to keep up with demand they make 200,000,000 Skittle candies every day!
- The inventor of peanut M&Ms never tried his own creation — he was allergic to peanuts.

STUFF YOU'LL NEED

- **36" cardboard mailing tube**
- **Paint** (whichever color or colors you like)
- **Masking tape or painter's tape**
- **String of holiday lights**

1. You can use this for Halloween or delivering goodie bags at parties. Paint the tube whichever color you like. (Orange for Halloween, your favorite sports teams' colors — anything!)
2. Attach the tube to the banister of a staircase. Try to avoid duct tape, as it might do some damage after peeling it off.
3. String the lights around the tube and banister.
4. Yell "Wee!" as you send candy down the slide to all your hungry friends.

DON'T TRY THIS AT HOME

BUILD YOUR OWN ROLLER COASTER

How amazing would it be to have a roller coaster in your backyard? Very. How dangerous would that be? Extremely. A long time ago, someone thought this would be a fun (and safe) thing for kids to build. No thanks, we'll stick with trips to Disney World.

Ultimate Pool Battle

How to build a floating ping-pong table.

DIFFICULTY LEVEL

STUFF YOU'LL NEED

- **3 Pool noodles**
- **Corrugated plastic sheet ¼" x 24" x 48"**
- **Two 10" x 1" stainless steel pan-head screws**
- **1 ½" x 2' PVC pipe**
- **One roll of 5 ½" black mesh ribbon**
- **Plastic ping-pong paddles and balls**

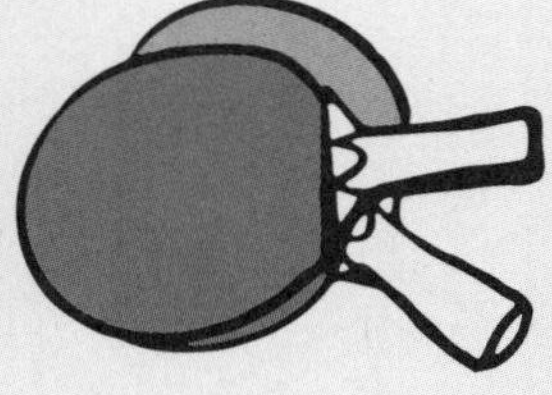

1 Cut two lengths of pool noodle to 24 inches and two to 48 inches.

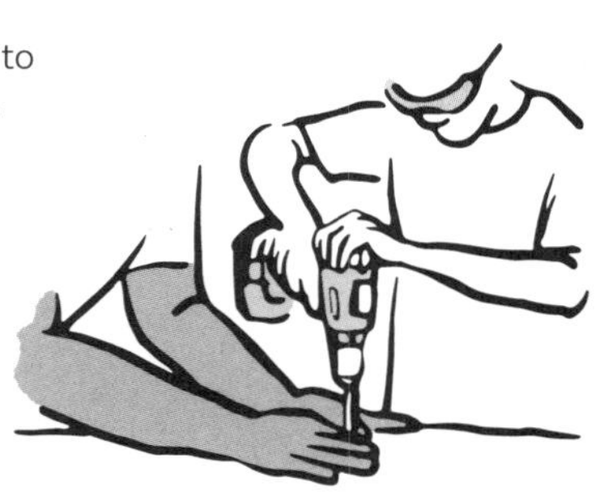

2 Find the centerline of the plastic sheet by measuring 24 inches in from the long end. Mark a point one inch in from either side on this line. With a cordless drill and a 9/64-inch twist bit, drill pilot holes in the two marks.

3 Use the same bit to drill holes in the base of each end cap. Place construction adhesive on the playing surface around the pilot holes and press each end cap in position. Drive a screw through the end cap and into the pilot hole.

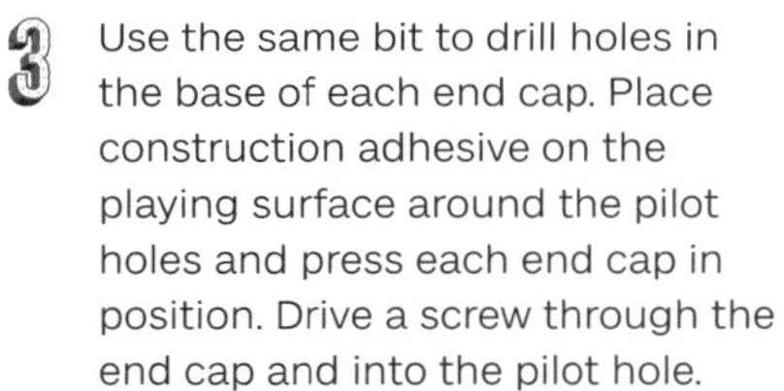

4 To form the net posts, measure and mark two pieces of PVC pipe to three inches long and cut. Press each one into an end cap mounted to the table.

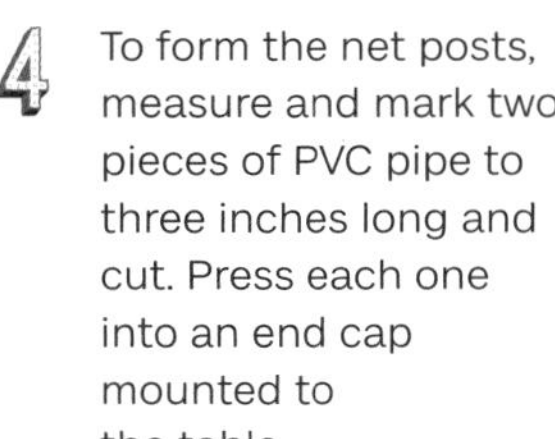

Cut a piece of black mesh ribbon to 27 inches long and three inches wide. Wind a little ribbon around one of the net posts, then use a hot-glue gun to attach the ribbon to the post. Extend the ribbon to the other side of the table. Wind the ribbon around the opposite post, and glue it in place. Press another end cap on top of each post.

[Note: You can also buy a ping-pong net online if you'd like to skip this part.]

Test-fit the pool noodles to the edges of the game board. Once you're sure they fit, glue each one to the board with construction adhesive. Drill ¼-inch-diameter drain holes near each corner of the playing surface.

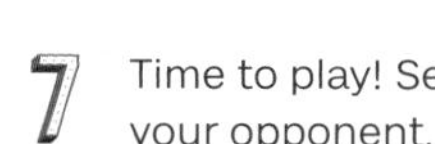

Time to play! Serve to your opponent.

OFFICIAL RULES OF PING-PONG

- Games are to 11 points
- Players get two serves each, then switch
- You don't have to be the server to win a point. Any mess-up earns a point for the opposite player.
- If a game ties at 10-10, you go into extra time and must win by two points. Each player takes turns with one serve until someone wins.
- In official competition, games are played best of five (first to win three games) or best of seven (first to win four games.)

Build a Handheld Water Cannon

Make a splash with this beast.

DIFFICULTY LEVEL

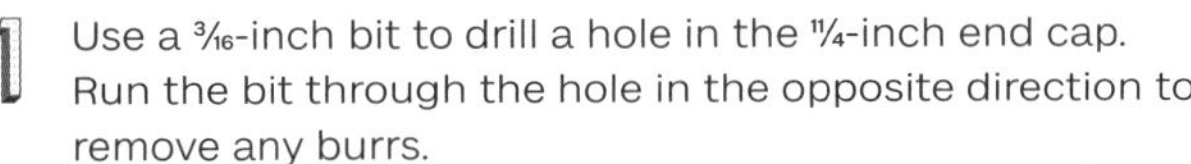

STUFF YOU'LL NEED

- **1 1" PVC pipe, 20" long**
- **1 1¼" PVC pipe, 20" long**
- **1 1" PVC end cap**
- **1 1¼" PVC end cap**
- **1 ¾" PVC plug**
- **PVC primer and cement**
- **3/16" drill bit**
- **3 No. 15 o-rings (1" outside diameter x ¾" inside diameter x 1 8" thick)**
- **Lubricant such as WD-40 or Vaseline**

1 Use a 3/16-inch bit to drill a hole in the 1¼-inch end cap. Run the bit through the hole in the opposite direction to remove any burrs.

2 Apply pipe cement primer to the inside of the 1¼-inch end cap and the last inch of the 1¼-inch barrel, followed by a thin film of cement.

3 Push the parts together and twist slightly to distribute the pipe cement evenly. Repeat step 2 and 3 for the end cap on the one-inch piston pipe.

4 On the other end of the piston pipe, use sandpaper or an abrasive sanding drum attached to your drill, until you've made enough room to fit the ¾-inch pipe plug into the pipe. About ¼ inch of the plug's stem should stick out.

5 Roll two o-rings onto the exposed part of the plug to form a base. Then roll the third ring on top of those. This will create a barrier that allows you to force water out the other end.

6 Apply a little lubricant to the o-rings. Pump the squirter gently a few times in a bucket of water to ensure that the rings are seated correctly. Let the soaking begin!

Make a Sword Bookmark

DIFFICULTY LEVEL

Save your spot with a totally sweet saber.

STUFF YOU'LL NEED

- **Craft sticks**
- **Colored glitter**
- **Glue**
- **Black paint**

1. Paint the bottom of the stick black. This will be the sword's handle.
2. Put a thin coat of glue on the unpainted section of the stick.
3. Sprinkle the glitter over the glue. (If you want to mimic a lightsaber, you can use green or blue for a Jedi, red if Darth Vader is your fave.)
4. Let dry and go to battle with your next book!

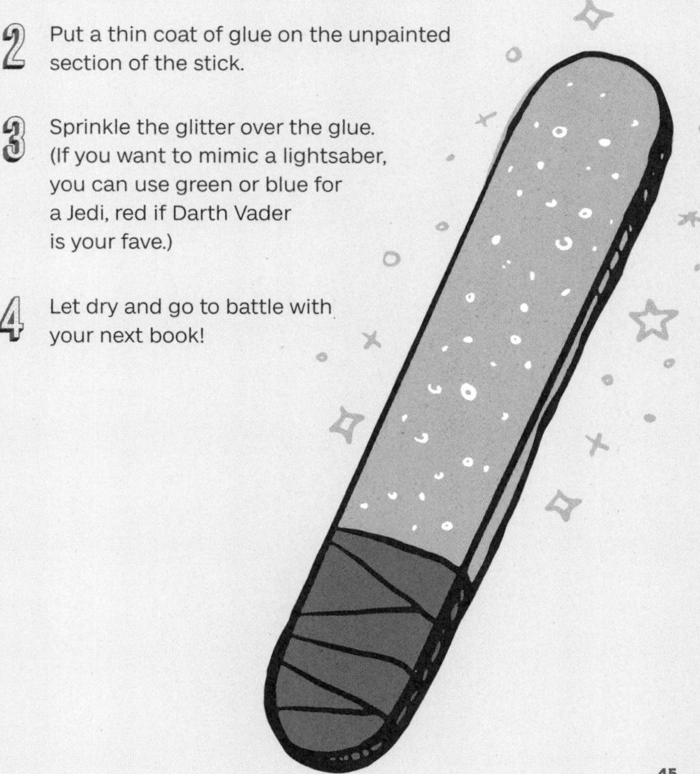

Create Your Own Tie-Dye T-Shirt

You won't need any tools, but you will need a workspace that can stand getting pretty messy.

STUFF YOU'LL NEED

- **Tie-dye kit** (Buying a kit is cheaper than buying all of the dyes separately.)
- **A white T-shirt**
- **Rubber bands**

1. If you are going to be dying a brand-new t-shirt, make sure you wash it in a washing machine first.
2. Prepare the area you'll be working on with waterproof drop clothes. (Warning: The dyes will easily stain wood and countertops.)
3. Soak the shirt in water and wring it out a bit.
4. There are many different patterns you can experiment with, but for your first one, pinch the middle of the shirt, and then twirl it around so it is shaped like a long roll of dough.

5 Starting at the top, wrap a rubber band around the roll. Repeat this, creating 5-6 sections.

6 Apply a different color to each section. Don't worry about coloring inside the lines — you'll get amazing results when the colors bleed.

7 Put the shirt in a plastic bag and let it soak. Follow the die kit directions, but the longer you leave it, the more intense the colors will be.

8 After the wait time is over, take the shirt to a sink or a hose outside. Rinse it until the water runs clear, then undo the rubber bands and marvel at your wearable work of art!

HOW TO SEW SOMETHING

KNOW THESE BASICS TO SEW ON A PATCH OR FIX A RIP

THREAD A NEEDLE

Measure the length of the area you want to sew, double it, and then add a few inches. Snip the thread to that length, then thread it through the eye (the hole) of the needle. Pull your thread through the needle until you have equal lengths on each side, then tie off the ends together. The knot will stop the thread from slipping through the fabric as you sew.

LEARN THE RUNNING STITCH

Poke the needle through both pieces of fabric, then push it back through the fabric a quarter-inch over. This creates one stitch. Continue to the end of the seam. To close the stitches, push the needle through the fabric without pulling the thread all the way through to create a loop. Run the needle back through the fabric and loop to create a knot. Repeat two to four times.

DID YOU KNOW?

Navy SEALs are elite warriors in America's military force who have to master an incredible number of skills to do what they do, and guess what? Learning how to sew is one of them!

THREE
THREE
THREE
UNLOCK YOUR
SUPERPOWERS
E=MC²
2+2=?
4×4=?

INTRODUCING

THE AMAZING YOU!

Every superhero has an origin story explaining how they got their powers. For example, Spider-Man was bitten by a radioactive spider, and the Hulk got blown up by a gamma bomb. The good news for you is that your superpower origin story will be a lot less painful — all it involves is reading this chapter! You are about to learn secrets to help you do things faster, incredible tricks to mesmerize your friends, and even some ideas to start making you some money! (Sorry, not billions of dollars like Iron Man has — you're going to have to read a much longer book to get that superpower.)

Terms You Should Know

- **ARTERY** Like a vein, except it carries blood away from your heart to other parts of your body. (p. 51)
- **ENTREPRENEUR** Someone who starts or runs a business. They can also be the founder. (see below) (p. 60)
- **FOUNDER** Someone who starts a company, like Steve Jobs at Apple, or Mr. Krabs, inventor of the Krabby Patty. (p. 56)
- **LITHIUM-ION** A type of rechargeable battery. (p. 56)
- **NEURON** Cells that send and receive signals from your brain. (p. 50)
- **WRITER'S BLOCK** When you are staring at a blank page and can't think of a single thing to write. (p. 62)
- **X-RAY VISION** A superpower that you absolutely will not have after you read this chapter.

13 MIND-BLOWING FACTS ABOUT YOUR BRAIN

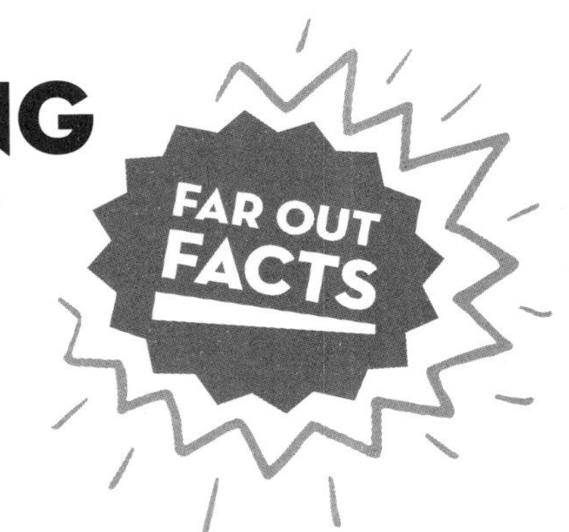

The inside secrets of how your noggin works.

1 The brain has three major parts, and they all have jobs:

- The cerebrum is the largest part, and it controls speech, learning, and motion.
- The cerebellum controls muscle movement and balance.
- The brainstem connects to your spinal cord and controls automatic things like your body temperature, your heart rate, and even sneezing. (So your cerebrum says, "Bless you!" when your brainstem sneezes!)

2 The cerebrum has two distinct halves, and oddly enough, the left side controls the right side of your body, and the right side controls the left.

3 To remember where the brain parts are located:

- cere**B**ellum is on the **b**ottom
- cereb**R**um is on the **r**oof

4 Doing crossword puzzles or similar games is proven to help increase your memory. That's right, playing Sudoku is like doing sit-ups for your noggin.

5 Snacking can help you get good grades! Foods like blueberries, nuts, oranges and pumpkin seeds have nutrients that help your brain remember things better.

6 Bigger isn't always better: An adult human brain weighs three pounds. A sperm whale's brain weighs about 20 pounds. But who do you think is better at multiplying fractions?

7 Unlike your phone, your brain's storage capacity is basically unlimited. Billions of neurons work

together to hold memories — scientists say it's about the equivalent of a million gigabytes. By comparison, the most powerful iPhone holds 1,000 gigabytes. And bonus: Your brain's screen never cracks.

8 Information travels in your brain at 268 MPH. Careful, remembering the answer on a history test can get you a speeding ticket!

9 Brain freeze is actually a type of headache. There is an artery junction at the back of your throat that pumps blood to your brain, and when it gets cold, it sends a pain signal to your brain. To help it pass quicker, press your tongue to the roof of your mouth to help warm it back up.

10 Your brain never gets a nap — it is always working even when you are asleep. (Sometimes they are working a lot more than we'd like when they create super-scary dreams!)

11 The brain is powerful — literally. It can generate enough to light up a lightbulb.

12 Having trouble concentrating? Drink some water. Even slight dehydration can make you feel foggy.

13 Don't ask an ancient Egyptian mummy for help with your math homework. Before they were placed in tombs, they had their brains removed through their noses.

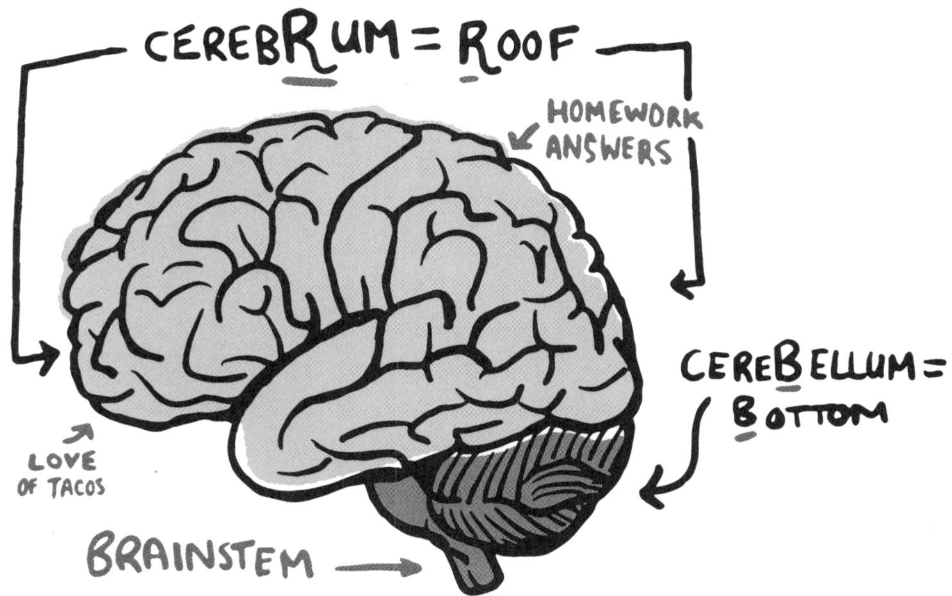

ABRACADABRA!

Learn these easy-to-master magic tricks.

DIFFICULTY LEVEL

Pick a Card, Any Card Trick

Correctly guess which card your audience member picked from the deck.

1. Shuffle the cards, proving you haven't set anything up.
2. With the cards facing away from you, fan them out and tell your audience member to pick a card and to keep it hidden from you.
3. Shuffle the cards again, and then split them, holding one half in each hand. Tell your audience member to place their card on top of the bottom half. Make a big show of you not looking at their card as they place it down, but while you're doing that, steal a glance at the bottom card of the top half.
4. Close the top half on the deck and be sure to remember that card!
5. Flip the deck over and fan it out smoothly on the table. Pick out the card directly to the right of the one you glanced at and ask, "Is this your card?"
6. Patiently wait for them to stop applauding.

The Levitating Card Trick

For a more amazing reveal, try this variation.

1. After you fan out the cards, split the fan in the middle between the card you peeked at and the card you know is their card. Collect the cards into two piles, keeping the audience member's card at the bottom of the pile on your right.
2. Place the pile to your left on top, making one pile again. Their card should be at the top of the deck now. Hold the deck up with the face of the bottom card facing your audience member.
3. Extend the index finger of your free hand over the deck, and twirl it around and say, "Rise, card! Rise!"
4. Place your index finger on top of the deck, and secretly extend your pinky to touch the back card. Move your hand up slowly, pushing the last card up with your pinky while making "Whoo!" noises.
5. Have a glass of water ready to splash on their face after they faint with astonishment!

Stretching Rainbows Illusion

They won't believe their eyes.

STUFF YOU'LL NEED

- A piece of cardboard or oak tag
- 1 large dinner plate
- 1 smaller dinner plate
- Markers
- Scissors

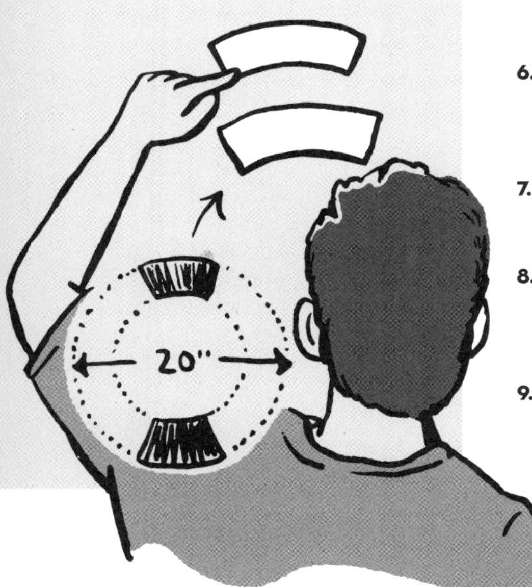

MAKE YOUR RAINBOWS

1. Trace a circle from the larger plate. Place the smaller plate inside the circle lining up the middle and trace the smaller plate.

2. Cut out the ring you've drawn and cut it into two exactly equal halves. Stack the halves on top of each other and cut a slight angle at each end.

3. You should now have two identical arches. Use the markers to color them as rainbows.

THE TRICK

4. Have your audience member stand next to you in front of a table. Let them examine the two rainbows, stacking them on top of each other to show they are the same exact size.

5. Place one down on the table, and then holding each end of the other one, pretend to strain as you pull and stretch it. (Note: Don't actually pull on it, or you'll rip it!)

6. Place the "stretched" one on the table below the other one (closer to the edge of the table you're standing behind). It will miraculously appear bigger than the other one.

7. Now pick up the "smaller" rainbow and repeat the fake stretching process. Place it below the other rainbow, and it will look bigger!

8. Pick up the "bigger" one, pretend to squeeze it back, and place it on top of the other rainbow, showing your audience that they are the same size again.

9. Feel like we forgot to tell you how to "do" the trick? Well, the truth is that you don't have to do anything! What's happening is an optical illusion. Your eye and your brain perceive the top arch as smaller, even though they are identical. Magic!

Math Mind Game

DIFFICULTY LEVEL

Correctly guess anyone's age and house address.

STUFF YOU'LL NEED

- Paper
- Pencil
- Calculator

1. Tell your audience member to write their house number on a piece of paper that you can't see. Then give them a calculator and tell them to follow your commands.
2. Double the house number.
3. Add five.
4. Multiply that number by 50.
5. Add their age.
6. Add the number of days in a year, then subtract 615.
7. Command them to show you the resulting number. Declare with confidence their age and address: the last two figures of the number will be their age, and the remaining numbers will be their house address.

Easy Bet: I Can Stick a Piece of Paper to the Wall Without Tape

DIFFICULTY LEVEL

No glue, no tape, no problem!

STUFF YOU'LL NEED

- **A pencil**
- **A sheet of paper**

1 Find a sucker — er, friend — who will accept a bet that you can stick a piece of paper to the wall with no adhesive.

2 Place the pencil on the sheet of paper, and holding one end, quickly wiggle it back and forth several times.

3 Slap the paper on the wall and watch it stick! The trick? The pencil is causing static electricity (the same thing that gives you a shock when you shuffle across a rug and touch a doorknob), which makes the paper cling to the wall.

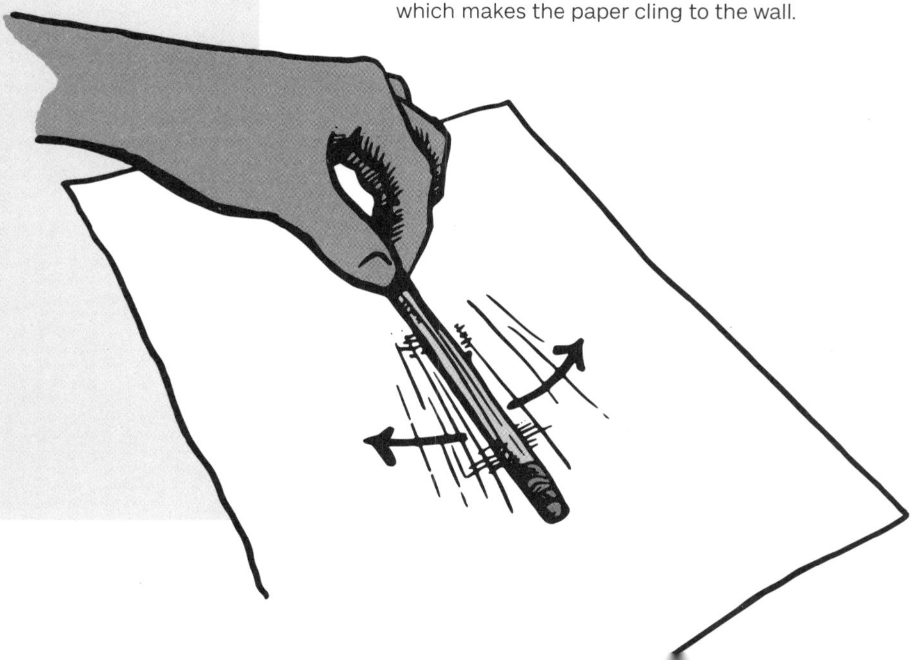

SCIENTISTS JUST FIGURED OUT HOW TO TURN YOUR BODY INTO A BATTERY

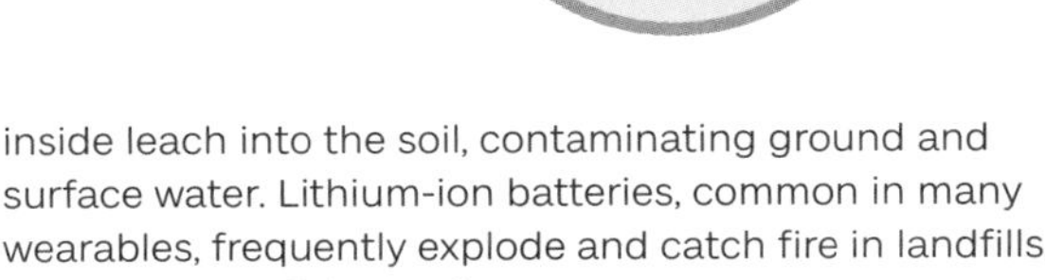

Imagine charging your phone — with yourself!

YOU KNOW THAT YOUR BODY needs to maintain a constant temperature of about 98.6 degrees Fahrenheit to stay healthy and functioning, right? Well to do that, it needs to regulate a balance between heat gain and heat loss. And in that process, scientists have measured that you lose a ton of energy.

That's where a tiny new wearable gadget called a thermoelectric generator (TEG) comes in. It can turn that lost body heat into electrical energy. TEGs use a difference in temperature—like your body's temperature compared to the temperature of the surrounding air—to turn that energy into power.

You won't be a human light switch just yet though. Researchers say that these wearables can generate only about one volt of energy for every square centimeter of skin space (That is less than the power of a AA or AAA battery.), but the possibilities are incredible. Imagine one day wearing an Apple Watch that charges itself?

Besides being super-convenient, not needing batteries is good news for the environment. Batteries use rare-earth metals and corrosive materials, and when batteries break down in landfills, the chemicals inside leach into the soil, contaminating ground and surface water. Lithium-ion batteries, common in many wearables, frequently explode and catch fire in landfills, releasing harmful greenhouse gases.

As the technology is studied and advanced, we can expect huge increases in power.

But scientists predict that we could see these body-powered wearables in stores in the next five to 10 years, so don't toss those charging chords just yet.

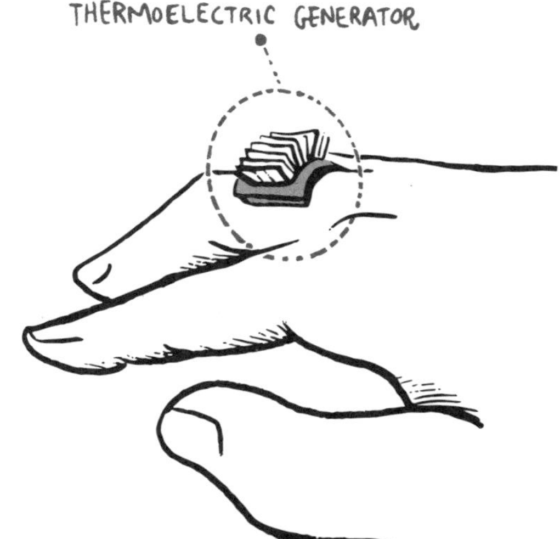

HUMAN POWERHOUSES

THESE FOLKS HAVE ENERGY TO SPARE!

WHEELED WONDER
Aaron James Fotheringham holds multiple records for wheelchair stunts, including the longest wheelchair ramp jump of 70 feet!

SPEEDSTER
Sprinter Usain Bolt is the world's fastest man who once ran 100 meters in 9.58 seconds. He hit 27.33 mph during his record-setting run! That's faster than a pig, a squirrel and even some dogs.

STRONGMAN
Zydrunas "The Big Z" Savickas has more than 20 world records for strength. Think you could beat his 1,155-pound deadlift?

UNSTOPPABLE
Keira D'Amato holds the American women's marathon record, running 26.2 miles in just over 2 hours and 19 minutes. That's an average of 5.3 minutes per mile.

DON'T TRY THIS AT HOME

FROM THE BAD IDEA FILES

MOTORCYCLE-POWERED PADDLE BOAT

Normally a paddle boat is powered by your legs and feet, but someone thought attaching a motorcycle would be even better. Sure, that would stop you from getting tired, but this idea seems a little overboard to us.

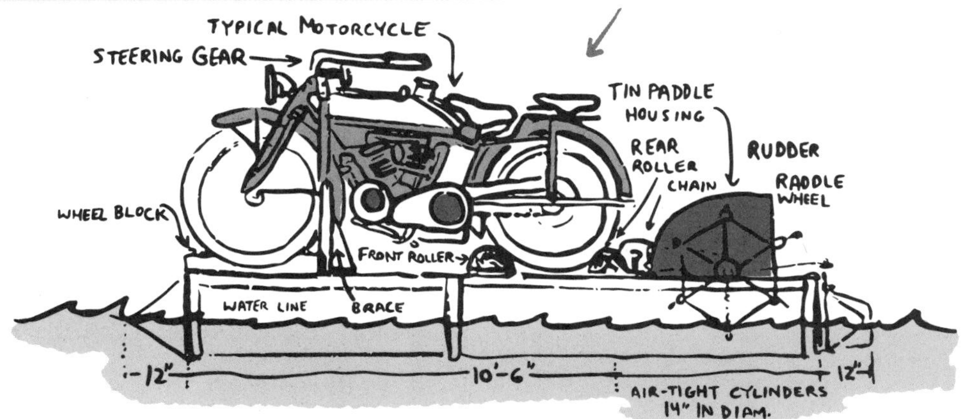

HOW TO
BUILD CONFIDENCE

Jonathan George, the founder of Rock My Campus, shares simple things you can do right now to be more confident.

1 **Write down 5-10 clear goals you want to accomplish this year.**

Start small. It can be something as simple as: make two close friends. Then ask yourself, how do I make those friends? Perhaps the steps would be to join a couple groups, classes, or clubs that interest you.

2 **Think about how you affect others.**

Have you ever tasted something that left a bad taste in your mouth? We can have the same effect on people — good or bad. Describe exactly how you want people to feel when they meet you. Then make sure you keep yourself accountable for how you interact with those around you. *For example: If I want people to feel seen, valued, loved, happy, and supported, I can't show up being rude and having a bad attitude.*

3 Be thoughtful about social media.

Social media can have a bad effect on your mental health. Here is a formula to help you keep it as a positive and fun part of your life:

"I am on [social media platform] because I love to [your favorite thing to do on it] so that I can [your best reaction.]"

For example: "I am on [TikTok] because I love to [watch funny cat videos] so that I can [share and laugh with my friends]."

A NAVY SEAL'S ADVICE FOR KEEPING CALM IN STRESSFUL SITUATIONS

FORMER ELITE U.S. MILITARY SNIPER BRANDON WEBB SHARES HIS TIPS FOR DEALING WITH PRESSURE

USE YOUR IMAGINATION
"When we are training for missions, we visualize it step by step in our minds. We rehearse what we are going to say, imagine what could go wrong and what we'd do about it. We do this so many times that if something does happen in real life, we're ready because it's like we've already done it."

BELIEVE IN YOUR ABILITIES
"Push through problems, don't ever give up. When Michael Phelps competed at the Beijing Summer Olympics, he dove into the pool and his goggles flooded with water. He was essentially swimming blind, but he trusted his training and swam on and won the race."

BE YOUR BIGGEST CHEERLEADER
"Positive self-talk — telling yourself you can do this — is something that really works. When I trained snipers in the Navy SEALs, we saw that trainees performed much better during target practice when they told themselves they were getting better, rather than concentrating on their misses."

HOW TO
Start Your Own Business

Marc Randolph, the co-founder of Netflix, helps you begin your life as an entrepreneur — make money and be your own boss!

THERE IS NO SUCH THING AS A GOOD IDEA

"Despite what anyone will tell you, there is no such thing as a good idea — they're all bad ideas. Netflix was a bad idea! The thing that is important is that whatever your business idea might be, you try it. And after you try it, you see what is working, not working, learn and adjust. Every single person that you've ever read about who has a successful company didn't spend all this time dreaming about their great idea. They figured out a way to test it today."

START WITH SOMETHING YOU UNDERSTAND

"I get a lot of people who come to me and say, 'Marc, I've got this great idea. It's going to be this box that you get into, and it instantly transports you across the country.' Well, that's a great idea, but unless you have some special expertise in teleportation, I'm not sure how you're going to be able to pull that off. So, if you love dogs and have experience with them, a dog walking business makes a lot of sense. But if you don't have any experience with dogs, you might want to try something else."

LOOK FOR PROBLEMS

"Rather than trying to convince someone that they need something, it's so much better to find someone who needs something and convince them that you are the person to help. Part of that is just listening and looking for a pain point, something that makes people frustrated. If you're hanging out at a barbecue, and you overhear an adult say, 'Oh man, one of the things I hate most is having to bring my garbage cans out to the end of the driveway every Tuesday night.' Your ears should perk up. Maybe there's an opportunity to start a business hauling people's garbage cans out for them. Same goes for raking leaves or anything people don't like to do."

SPREAD THE WORD

"Once you have your business idea, tell as many people as possible. Even someone who doesn't have garbage cans or a lawn to rake. Chances are they know someone who could use your services."

DON'T BE AFRAID TO ASK FOR HELP

"The most powerful thing you can ever do is admit you don't know something. It's like magic. People want to help you, I promise. If you say, 'I don't understand,' people will explain. If someone doesn't buy from you, ask, 'What could I have done differently next time?' People want to help you succeed."

GREAT BUSINESS IDEAS FOR KIDS

Kim Perell, founder of the Side Hustle Accelerator, shares her picks for businesses you can launch.

Pet watching, walking and washing (we love pets!)

Making and selling crafts, candles and cards

Car washing

Babysitting

Yard cleanup

WHERE DO GREAT IDEAS COME FROM?

Artists and innovators share the secrets of creativity.

"You don't need directions, just point yourself to the top and go!"

DWAYNE "THE ROCK" JOHNSON, Actor, wrestler, business owner

"The only advice anybody can give is if you want to be a writer, keep writing. And read all you can, read everything."

STAN LEE, Marvel Comics legend

"My mother instilled in me the idea that creativity starts with taking a leap of faith — telling your fears they are not allowed where you are headed."

BEYONCE, Musician

"...be creative without worrying about being perfect."

DAV PILKEY, Author of *Captain Underpants*

"I don't believe in writer's block. There are good days when you're writing and less good days. I've learned that if it's not happening to walk away and return later. I doodle a lot and often get my best ideas with a pencil in my hand while I'm doodling. The problem is, sometimes I lose my doodles and that's bad!"

JUDY BLUME, Author of *Tales of a Fourth Grade Nothing and* many others

"You can't use up creativity. The more you use, the more you have."

MAYA ANGELOU, Award-winning poet

"I think it is possible for ordinary people to choose to be extraordinary."

ELON MUSK, Head of Tesla and SpaceX

"The most important thing about creativity is that you honor your creativity, and you don't ever ignore it or go against what that creative image is telling you."

LADY GAGA, Musician

"Imagination is more important than knowledge. Knowledge is limited. Imagination encircles the world."

ALBERT EINSTEIN, Scientist

"The one thing that you have that nobody else has is you. Your voice, your mind, your story, your vision. So, write and draw and build and play and dance and live only as you can."

NEIL GAIMAN, Author of *Coraline* and many others

"The best tip I could give you is to be active. So many people talk about what they want to do, and they just love words. Put actions behind your words. Don't be a talker, be a doer."

KEVIN HART, Actor and comedian

HOW TO MEDITATE

Many great artists and innovators say that meditation is a wonderful way to clear your mind of clutter so you can find great ideas. There are tons of great apps that instruct you on meditating, but here is a simple way from Brigham and Women's Hospital in Boston to get started:

- Find a quiet place and sit in a comfortable chair or on the floor.
- Set a gentle sound timer on your phone for one minute. (You can increase the time as you get in the swing of things.)
- Close your eyes and begin breathing in through your nostrils and out through your mouth. Concentrate on your breath, feel your belly rise and fall.
- Try to clear your mind, but when thoughts come up, don't fight them. Simply note that these thoughts came in, then watch them drift away and return to your breathing.
- When the timer buzzes, get up slowly.

As weird as it sounds, it is hard to sit there and think about nothing. Start with just three minutes, and build up the amount of time slowly.

REAL LIFE ADVENTURE

CHECK OUT THESE SUPERHEROES IN ACTION!

You don't have to wear a cape to save the day.

DINER DISASTER AVERTED

While eating in a restaurant with his girlfriend one typical Friday night, 16-year-old Chase Eller saw something that was anything but typical: a baby choking on their food. The baby's mother was panicking, so without thinking twice, Chase jumped into action. He ran to the baby and performed the Heimlich Maneuver (abdominal thrusts that help clear a blocked airway) which he learned in his health class. The move worked and saved the baby's life. Afterward, Chase told a reporter he was happy he was there to help, adding, "The baby was smiling at me." The baby was happy too!

SUPER KITTY!

Police officers see a lot of crazy things, but this has to be at the top of the list for officer Patrick Daugherty. After a 911 call was made to police dispatch and no one was heard on the line, officer Daugherty was sent to the home of Gary Rosheisen in Ohio. The officer found Gary sprawled on the ground, next to his wheelchair, and Gary's cat, Tommy, next to the phone! After receiving medical care, Gary explained that he tried teaching Tommy how to hit the speed dial button for 911 in case of an emergency but had no idea if the cat understood. Well, Tommy sure did! "He's my hero," Gary told reporters after the incident.

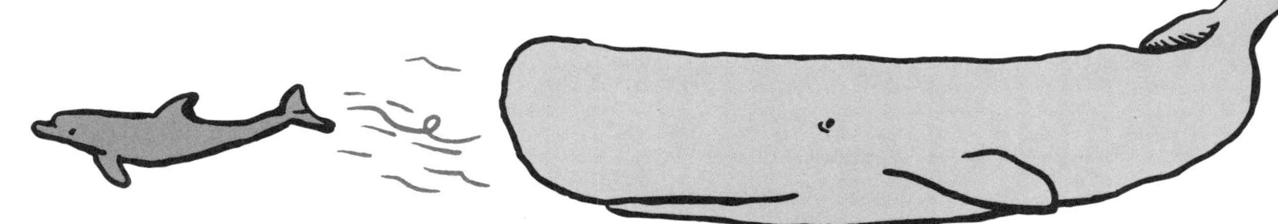

A WHALE-Y GOOD FRIEND

It was a sad and frustrating situation when a sperm whale and her calf got stuck on a sandbar off the coast of New Zealand. People could not figure out how to help the poor animals get free, but luckily a bottlenose dolphin nicknamed Moko swam by and saved the day. Moko zipped over to the whales and onlookers watched him guide them through a channel that led out to the deeper water. Best swim buddy ever!

TODDLER TO THE RESCUE

When Aaron Haynes had a terrible accident with a wood chisel, he was in real danger of dying. The chisel hit an artery in his arm, and he was losing blood fast. Lucky, his 3-year-old son AJ quickly picked up a phone and dialed 911. His quick action saved his dad's life and earned him a place in the Guinness Book of World Records as the youngest person to make a life-saving phone call.

QUICK-THINKING LIFESAVERS

After hearing a big crash in the dining kitchen, three children ran in to find their mother, Ashley Eggleston, lying on the floor and unresponsive. The kids heard a car passing by and ran outside screaming for help. The car stopped and friends Emilee Tikka, 16, Eva Sarkinen, 16 and Kate Nylund, 15, jumped out to help. They called 911 and the dispatcher explained how to perform CPR. Eva did CPR for about four minutes until first responders arrived and were able to get Ashley safely to the hospital. The group of kids and the thankful mom say that they have become like one big family from that day on.

MINI BATMAN

Five-year-old Caleb Bale's nickname is Caleb Batman, and wow did he earn it. While his mother was driving, she experienced a terrible seizure. Caleb, who was napping in the back seat, woke up, unbuckled his belt, climbed up into the driver's seat, and steered the car to safety! He flagged down a passing car, whose driver called 911 and got his mom the help she needed. Get this kid a Batmobile!

GET YOUR HOMEWORK DONE FASTER

Elizabeth Fraley, is an expert teacher who runs Kinder Ready and Elementary Wise. Here are her helpful tips to make homework easier.

MAKE YOURSELF A SCHEDULE

Think about a horror movie — someone is walking down a dark hallway and suddenly a monster pops up around the corner. Freaky, right? When we don't know what is coming, it can be scary and stressful. That's why one of Elizabeth's top pieces of advice is making a weekly or monthly schedule so you know what is coming up (i.e., a math test on Friday.) With it written down, you are less likely to wake up in the middle of the night on Thursday screaming, "I forgot to study!"

PICK YOUR SPOT

Speaking of horror, famous author Stephen King, who has written more than 60 spooky novels, says one of the keys to cranking out book after book is that he has a specific room that he only uses to write in. He doesn't play video games or read the newspaper there — when he sits in that chair, it tells his brain that it is time to work. Pick a homework spot for yourself. Maybe it is a desk, maybe it is your kitchen table. Wherever is comfortable to sit and spread out your books and papers, do your work in that same spot every day and it will help get you in the "get work done" mindset quicker.

TAKE BREAKS

You might not realize this, but you have completed a marathon. That's right, 26.2 miles. Congrats! Here's the thing: you didn't do it all at once. Maybe you cruised a mile in gym class one day, maybe you traveled another mile in the mall another day — that big 26.2 mile number was broken into pieces, making it more doable. Elizabeth says that if it is hard to sit at your desk for an hour or more doing homework, try this method: Use your phone's timer to help you track 25 minutes of work and five minutes of breaktime. Repeat the on and off time until you get your workload done.

MAKE A TO-DO LIST

Make a list of things you need to do: study for a math test, write a book report, things like that. Some days the list will look a little bigger than others, but one thing is true: There is nothing more satisfying than crossing something out once it is finished. In your face, geometry quiz!

START WITH THE EASY STUFF

Ever hear the expression "low-hanging fruit?" The idea is that fruit on the low branches is easier to pick and eat than fruit on branches that require a ladder to reach. So, look at your to-do list. Is there anything you can bang out super-fast and easy? Do those first. Once you get some momentum, you'll be like a boulder picking up speed as it rolls down a hill. Look out!

NO BANGING YOUR HEAD AGAINST THE DESK ALLOWED

No matter how smart you are or how well you pay attention in school, there will be assignments that are tough. Frustration is a natural reaction, but rather than driving yourself nuts trying to figure it out, Elizabeth suggests that you write down everything you do know and leave a note for your teacher: "I am stuck on what to do next." This way your teacher knows that you put in real effort, and also lets them know the specific part you need help with. "I can't do this math problem" is a lot harder to help someone with than "I don't understand how to multiply these two fractions."

SLEEP!

No, not while you are doing homework. But all kinds of scientific studies show that a big key to focusing and problem-solving is rest. Ideally, you should be getting eight to 12 hours of sleep a night. (And no, games or watching TikTok on your phone until two in the morning in bed does not count as sleep!)

BIG BRAINS = BIG MONEY

The record holder for highest winnings during a regular season Jeopardy! game is Ken Jennings, who raked in $2,520,700 after winning 74 games! Ken was such a popular player that he is now one of the two hosts of the show. Amy Schneider is the second-place record holder for the most wins — 40!

AMAZING MEMORIZATION SECRETS

Use these tricks to train your brain to remember better.

CONNECT THE DOTS

Remembering a fact like water freezes at 32 degrees Fahrenheit might be tough, but connecting it to something you know, like Shaquille O'Neal's jersey number was 32, could help. Imagine Shaq shivering in his number 32 jersey, and you'll never forget that freezing number! And the connection could be anything: your friend's birthday, your grandma's house number, digits in a phone number, etc.

STUDY AND THEN SNORE

Scientific studies show that your brain remains hard at work while you are sleeping, so it is a good idea to review any info you are trying to memorize right before you hit the pillow.

SPEAK AND SPELL

Another way to further embed info in your noggin is to write things out. And even better, say them out loud as you write. Science shows that when your brain is thinking about something, and also commanding your hand to spell it out and your mouth to say it, it can be a triple-whammy of a memory trick.

THE POWER OF FIRST LETTERS

Something called "mnemonics" (pronounced new-mon-icks) are tricks to help you remember a series of words in order. For example, if you are trying to remember the names of the Great Lakes, in order, think of this phrase: SuperMan Helps EveryOne. From west to east, the five lakes are: Superior, Michigan, Huron, Erie and Ontario.

BUILD A MEMORY PALACE

This is a weird one, but people who compete in memory competitions swear it works. The idea is that you picture a structure you are very familiar with, like the inside of your house or school. Then in your head, you place the things you are trying to remember in it. The weirder, the better. So, if you are trying to remember the first presidents of the United States, put them in your kitchen. George Washington is sitting at the table, John Adams is raiding the fridge, Thomas Jefferson is making scrambled eggs at the stove. Memory experts say it is easier to recall visual images than facts that are just floating around your head.

Top Mnemonic Devices

The order of the colors of the rainbow

Roy G. Biv

Red, Orange, Yellow, Green, Blue, Indigo, Violet

The order of the planets

My Very Excellent Mom Just Served Us Nachos

Mercury, Venus, Earth, Mars, Jupiter, Saturn, Uranus, Neptune

The names of the five oceans

APples In Apple Sauce

Atlantic, Pacific, Indian, Arctic, Southern

The names of the continents

Eat An Apple As A Nice Snack

Europe, Antarctica, Australia, Asia, Africa, North America, South America

HOW TO GET ON TEEN JEOPARDY!

Wanna put your smarts to the ultimate TV test and make tons of dough?

Here's everything you need to know about getting famous and rich on one of the most popular game shows of all time.

AGE You need to be 13-17 years old to be eligible to apply for Teen Jeopardy!

REGISTER Set up a MyJeopardy! Account and complete the contestant registration.

TEST TIME Pass a 50-question online test and you will move past the first round. You can take it once a year in one of two ways: The first is called the Jeopardy! Test, which happens at a specific time that you get alerted to via email. The other is the Anytime Test, which, just like it sounds, allows you to log in and take it whenever is convenient.

WAITING GAME You get confirmation that your test has been submitted within 24 hours of taking it. Unlike school, you don't get alerted if you fail. But if you pass and meet all requirements, the Jeopardy! Contestant department will contact you for an audition.

AUDITION There are two parts to this. In the first round, you will take another 50-question online test in real-time via video conference. In the second part, you will play a mock version of the game against other hopeful contestants. At the end of the mock game, you will be asked to tell a little bit about yourself: things you like, don't like, your hobbies, funny family stories, etc.

WAIT AGAIN If you pass the test and do well at your audition, you will be placed in a pool of potential contestants for 18 months after your audition date. If you get picked, the show will reach out to you and tell you when to head out to California to compete on TV!

4
ART
ATTACK!

BRUSH UP ON YOUR CREATIVE SKILLS!

They say that humans have been making art since the dawn of history. (We don't know about you, but at dawn we're usually still sleeping!) Anyway, the point is that people — and even some animals — have an incredibly strong desire to make art. Why? Because it is fun, sometimes you get to make a mess, and you wind up with something that looks cool! Whether paint, video, music or writing is your thing, we hope you will find a project in this chapter that inspires you to let out your inner creative genius. (But just make sure your inner creative genius comes home in time for dinner — it's pizza night!)

Terms You Should Know

- **CELEBRITY** What you're destined to become once you unleash your art on the world.
- **ESPORTS** Short for electronic sports, they are organized gaming competitions. (p. 72)
- **GLYCERIN** A colorless, odorless, thick liquid that is sweet. (p. 83)
- **SELF-PUBLISH** When an author publishes their own book rather than having a big company doing it.

THINGS YOU DIDN'T KNOW ABOUT MOVIES, MUSIC, BOOKS AND GAMING

FAR OUT FACTS

COOL

WHOA!

1 To infinity and beyond a bad mess up: *Toy Story 2* almost didn't get released. Not because the folks at Pixar didn't like it — because an animator accidentally deleted most of it! Luckily, the movie's technical director had a backup on her computer at home.

2 In *Jurassic Park*, when confronted by a very hungry T. Rex, Dr. Grant advises, "Don't move! He can't see us if we don't move." It worked in the movie, but in real life, most paleontologists believe T. Rex had great vision and would gobble you up whether you ran or sat there like a screaming snack.

3 In an early version of *Star Wars: A New Hope*, R2-D2 spoke English instead of in beeps and bloops. And apparently, was kind of a jerk and bully to poor C-3PO!

4 When J.K. Rowling was in the middle of writing Harry Potter, she often had ideas pop into her head at random moments and would scramble to find something to write them down on. Her most unusual? She tweeted: "The best thing I ever wrote on was an aeroplane sick bag. Came up with the Hogwarts houses on it."

5 Minecraft was almost called "Cave Game" before its creator changed his mind. Hard to imagine over 130 million people playing "Cave Game" each month.

6 Esports is not only fun, but it also makes a ton of money. In 2021, esports generated over $1 billion! Next time you get in trouble for playing too many video games, simply explain that you are training to be a billionaire.

7 Taylor Swift holds the current record for the most No.1 hits on the U.S. Digital Song Sales chart. As of January 2022, she had 23 singles reach the top spot!

8 Dwayne "The Rock" Johnson doesn't just make great art by way of his movies, he *is* art. He has a tattoo that stretches across his chest, back and left arm. Given how big his muscles are, it took 60 hours to complete the tat!

9 You might have noticed that Dav Pilkey, creator of *Captain Underpants*, has a unique spelling for his first name. He revealed in an interview that when he was working at a Pizza Hut, his manager made him a name tag. The "e" on the label maker was broken and so, he explained, "My name tag said D-A-V, and it's just stuck."

10 In *The Avengers*, Bruce Banner has to get really angry to turn into the big green Hulk. But in the very first *Incredible Hulk* comic book, the thing that transformed him was the glow of moonlight. And he turned gray, not green!

11 The popularity of *The Avengers* is too big to be contained on Earth — NASA sent a digital version to the International Space Station for astronauts and space engineers to watch.

12 Kidz Bop has been around for more than 20 years, and the group's most famous member was singer-actress Zendaya.

13 Imagine if LeBron James' teammate in *Space Jam 2* was named "Happy Rabbit." That was Bugs Bunny's original name, until animators started calling him as "Bugs' Bunny," after Ben "Bugs" Hardaway who was the first person to direct a "Happy Rabbit" cartoon.

14 For a quick minute, the president of Nintendo wanted cute little Pikachu to have big muscles and be totally buff! The thinking was that this would make him more appealing to U.S. gamers. Bench press, I choose you!

15 Humans aren't the only animals who like to create art. Elephants in Thailand have been trained to paint pictures on canvases, and some of their work has sold for thousands of dollars! Guess these artists don't work for peanuts.

16 The world's oldest known cave painting was recently discovered in Indonesia: a life-sized picture of a pig that was made at least 45,500 years ago! That is some old bacon.

How to Make an Animated Movie *(with the Corner of Your Notebook)*

DIFFICULTY LEVEL

Before there were Pixar movies, there were flipbooks. Here are the simple steps to doodle your own motion picture.

STUFF YOU'LL NEED

- **A notebook or notepad**
- **A dark pen or pencil**

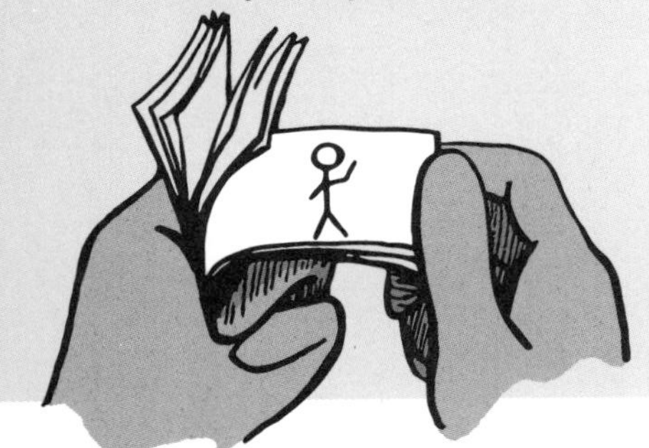

DID YOU KNOW?

Before computers, animated movies were drawn and painted by hand. It takes 12 drawings for just one second of film. So, a two-hour movie needs 86,000 drawings! Is anyone's hand cramping up just thinking about that?

The key to animation is tricking your brain with an optical illusion. If your eye sees a series of drawings that change slightly in quick succession, your brain interprets them as a moving image. Here is a super-simple way to get the concept and once you nail it, you can expand to create all kinds of cool adventures with multiple moving objects, people and monsters.

1. On the last page of your notebook, draw a stick figure with its arms pointing down.

2. Put the next blank page down, and trace over your stick figure, but draw one of the arms sticking out slightly higher.

3. Continue to draw 10-15 more pages, each time raising the arm until it is over its head.

4. Now draw five or so more pages, with the upright arm moving slightly to the right and slightly to the left.

5. Pinching the pages between your forefinger and thumb, flip through the pages and look down. Your stick figure is waving hello!

Design Your Own Car Cartoon Character

DIFFICULTY LEVEL

Inventing your own cartoon characters is super-fun. Speech bubbles are a great way to reveal your character's attitude ("Time to go fast!"), and there are little things you can do with your drawing that help show its emotions. Take a look at these examples and try working them into your own creations!

SHY GUY

Got a quiet, nervous character in mind? Make their eyes look up and inward and the hood bow down (like a puppy dog who is afraid they are in trouble.) Also try having the wheels go in slightly different directions, like someone whose legs are nervously shaking.

MAD DOG

Want to invent a villain (or a car that's just in a bad mood)? Draw crinkled down eyebrows, like a hungry animal searching for prey. Add big, sharp teeth and rugged tires leaning out like they just ran over something. Get outta the way, this monster doesn't have brakes!

SPEED DEMON

If your character loves to drive fast, here's how to make them look super-speedy and excited. Give them a big grill smile, make their eyes wide open (like someone excited to open a present), and give them big ol' tires that are ready to rip!

Swinging Sand Art

Use physics to make a wild design.

DIFFICULTY LEVEL

STUFF YOU'LL NEED

- **1 empty 20 oz. plastic bottle**
- **2 pounds of colored sand**
- **String**
- **Masking tape**
- **Construction paper**
- **Spray adhesive**

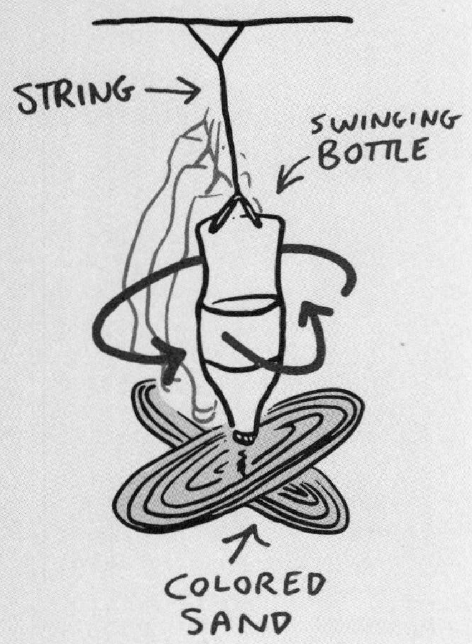

Lissajous figures are patterns that occur when something like a pendulum swings and then starts to spiral as it slows down.

1. Cut off the bottom of the plastic bottle, then poke three holes around the bottom of the bottle and one in the bottle cap.
2. Tie a six-inch piece of string in each hole, and then tie those to the main pendulum string. The main string should allow the bottle to hang an inch or so off the ground.
3. Cover the ground beneath the setup with construction paper. Spray the paper with adhesive if you want to keep your creation.
4. Using something sturdy above the paper, tie both ends of a string to end up with a hanging U shape. Tie the end of the pendulum string to the midpoint of the U.
5. Put a piece of masking tape over the hole in the cap, then fill most of the bottle with sand. Remove the tape and quickly put your finger over the hole.
6. Hold the bottle near the edge of the paper, then push it in a circular direction as you let go.
7. Watch amazing patterns form as the bottle swings and spins. Allow the adhesive to dry then brush off the excess sand. Physics art!

Lights, Camera, Flip Upside Down!

DIFFICULTY LEVEL

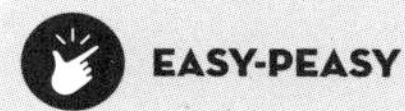

How to build a pinhole camera.

STUFF YOU'LL NEED

- **An empty shoebox and its lid**
- **A thumbtack**
- **Tape**
- **Wax paper or tracing paper**

1. Measure the center of the short side of the box and poke a hole in it.

2. On the opposite short side, find the center and measure a 2-foot x 2-inch box. Use scissors or a hobby knife to carefully cut it out.

3. Tape down the tracing or wax paper inside the box to cover the box hole.

4. Take your pinhole camera into a dark room and turn on a single lamp. Point the pinhole at the lamp and look at the wax paper box. You'll see an image of the lamp, upside down!

5. Why did it flip? Because light travels in a straight line. When the light from the top of the lamp passes through the pinhole, it continues in a straight line and ends up at the bottom of the paper.

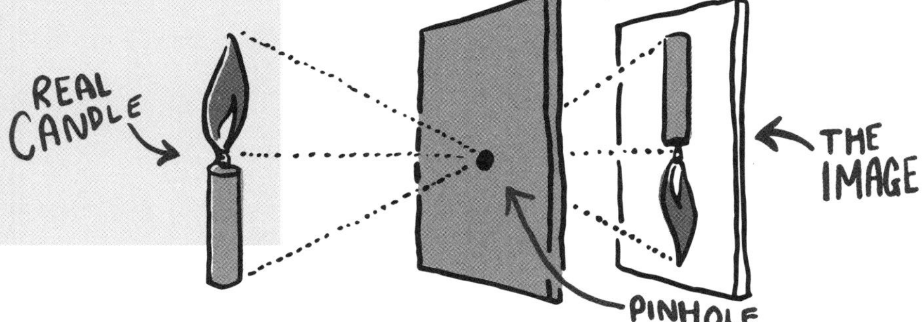

Turn Your Backyard Into a MOVIE THEATER

The gadgets you need — and the perfect spot to place them for the ideal outdoor cinematic experience.

STUFF YOU'LL NEED

- **A digital projector**
- **A laptop or tablet you can connect with a HDMI cord**
- **A Bluetooth speaker**
- **A sheet or blank wall**
- **A subscription to a streaming service like Netflix or Disney+**

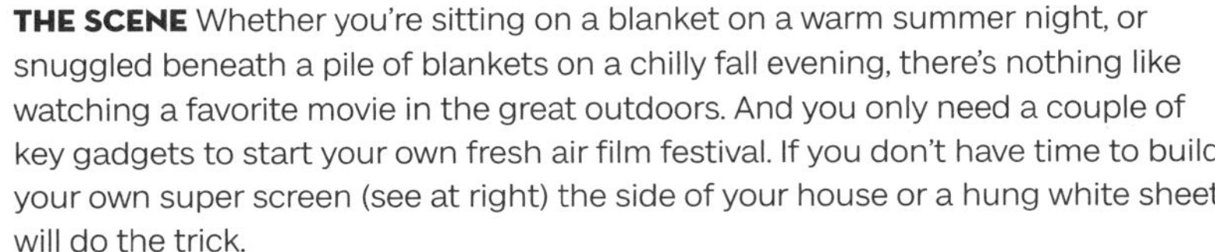

THE SCENE Whether you're sitting on a blanket on a warm summer night, or snuggled beneath a pile of blankets on a chilly fall evening, there's nothing like watching a favorite movie in the great outdoors. And you only need a couple of key gadgets to start your own fresh air film festival. If you don't have time to build your own super screen (see at right) the side of your house or a hung white sheet will do the trick.

Follow these pointers to create the perfect cinema under the stars. (Sorry, there's no gadget to make the sun set so you can start the movie faster!)

A Unless you're using a rear projector, it's best to screen at dusk, or if you're screening at sunset, set up so the sun sets behind the screen to avoid glare.

B Set speakers in front of the screen or right beside it, so the voices feel as if they are coming from the characters, not the woods around them.

C Where there's light, there are bugs. Make sure you put citronella candles or zappers (quiet ones) near your projector and screen to keep the picture free of flappy shadows. You can spritz equipment with bug spray.

D When it's dark and there's a movie playing the last place people are looking is down at their feet. Prevent trips and falls by taping down and tucking in wires.

Make a Super Screen

A sheet or wall will work fine, but a wrinkle-free surface will really make movie night pop.

DIFFICULTY LEVEL

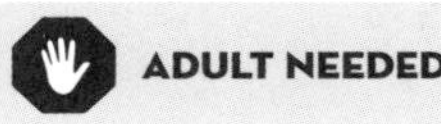

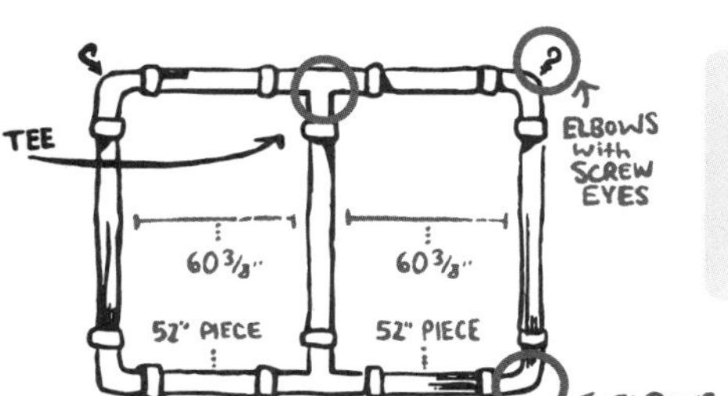

STUFF YOU'LL NEED

- One 33' length of ¾" PVC pipe
- Four ¾" PVC elbows
- Two ¾" PVC tee fittings
- Two 2" stainless-steel screw eyes
- One 57" X 101" white stretch fabric
- Thin rope

1. Sew four pockets into the stretchable fabric (see diagram). Notice that a 2-inch-wide unsewn gap is centered in the fabric's long edges. You'll need this gap to insert a PVC tee fitting.
2. Cut three pieces of PVC to 60 ⅜ inches and four to 52 inches.
3. With a ⅛-inch drill bit, have your adult helper drill a pilot hole at the corner point of the two PVC elbows for the screw eyes.
4. Slide the four 52-inch pieces of pipe into the fabric pockets. Insert a tee into the unsewn gap at the top and bottom of the frame and push each pipe into the horizontal socket of each tee.
5. Insert a 60-inch piece of pipe into the vertical socket of the top and bottom tee.
6. Slide four elbows onto the ends of the 52-inch-long pieces. The two elbows with screw eyes are positioned at the frame's top.
7. Insert the remaining two 60-inch pieces of pipe into the elbow sockets to complete the frame.
8. Attach the rope to the elbow screws and hang it up.

MOVIES MADE FOR THE GREAT OUTDOORS

A playlist to get your backyard movie marathon started.

- *Avatar*
- *The Goonies*
- *Jumanji*
- *Over the Hedge*
- *Paddington 2*
- *Raiders of the Lost Ark*
- *The Wizard of Oz*

HOW A SUPER FAN BUILT A CUSTOM-MADE 5-FOOT-LONG STAR DESTROYER

IT'S HARD TO SAY IF CHARLES ANDERSON is a bigger fan of Star Wars or of LEGOs. The professional animator spent more than 500 hours building a 44-pound, five-foot-long LEGO version of the Imperial Star Destroyer that is made up of nearly 20,000 bricks. Can you imagine the size of the box it came in?

Well, keep imagining because the box doesn't actually exist. See, not only did Charles build this amazing plastic creation, he designed the one-of-a-kind model himself!

Charles used a computer program called Studio 2.0 that allowed him to model out the entire ship on screen before he snapped a single brick together.

As a collector and maker of homemade Star Wars props (he also made a life-size replica of Han Solo trapped in carbonite), Charles was obsessive about making sure his LEGO Star Destroyer would be as close to the one in the film as possible. The ship has a unique shape (like an acute triangle), so precision with the structure's angles was super-important. "I decided at the beginning I wanted the whole thing to be five feet long," says Charles. "That triggered a lot of the other choices I had to make about proportions."

He started with a 3D scan of the A New Hope Imperial Star Destroyer and overlaid it into Studio 2.0 to design the skeleton of his build.

Once he had the hull mapped out, he moved on to the specifics. "Of the 15 months I spent designing and building this thing, most were spent in this software," he says. He jumped back and forth a lot between making the cool-looking parts of the model — like the cannons — and making the superstructure underlying it all. "Every time I designed something, I had to find places to hook it together," he explains. "I just hoped it would stick without breaking apart."

After 11 months, Charles's design was finished, and Studio 2.0 gave him list of almost 20,000 individual bricks that he would need to build the structure. He then used another program called BrickStock, which is connected to a database of every type of individual brick the LEGO Group has ever produced. (LEGO has more than 3,400 unique plastic pieces in over 60 colors on record— that's a lot of bricks!)

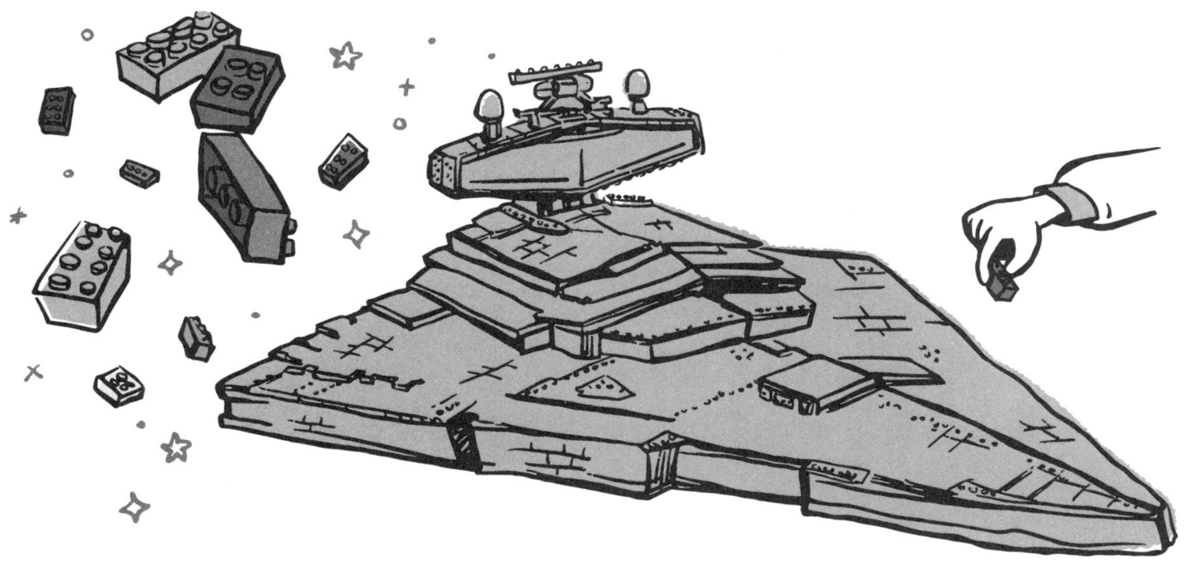

Using BrickStock, Charles found he already had about 8,500 of the 20,000 required destroyer pieces from various LEGO sets and lots he'd collected at garage sales and online marketplaces. He purchased some remaining parts from online sellers.

As Charles's bricks poured in, he started assembling his destroyer using the massive 3,300-page custom instruction book provided by Studio 2.0. But by page 200, he says, "things started to fall apart."

The engine end broke apart multiple times, and he explains that, "I had all these sharp angles that worked perfectly in my computer model, but refused to stick together in reality, and the tip of the model sagged at the bottom."

But like Luke Skywalker storming the Death Star in his X-Wing fighter, Charles refused to give up despite all of the problems. And 15 months later, he finally finished his five-foot-long LEGO masterpiece.

While his model isn't for sale, you can purchase his gargantuan instruction booklet, plus a list of the LEGOs you need. If you are up for the challenge (and have access to 20,000 LEGO bricks), may the force be with you!

GET INTO THE SPOOKY ZONE

Whether it's for Halloween or your latest scary TikTok, here are three easy — and freaky — decoration projects.

Homemade Zombie Pit

DIFFICULTY LEVEL

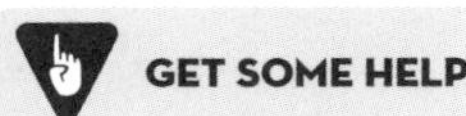

GET SOME HELP

STUFF YOU'LL NEED

- **A wooden pallet**
- **Some chains**
- **Arms, hands and heads from the Halloween store**
- **Cardboard and paint**

1. Place the pallet where you want your pit to be.
2. Wrap the chains around it, like you are locking down a hatch door.
3. Position the arms, hands and faces to make it look like they are trying to escape.
4. Add a hand-painted sign: "Zombie Pit — Stay Away!" (or depending on your mood, "Zombie Pit — Come In and Play!")

DIY Fog Machine

DIFFICULTY LEVEL

STUFF YOU'LL NEED

- **A gallon of distilled water**
- **A bottle of Glycerin** *(you can find at most drug stores)*
- **The top of a two-liter plastic soda bottle**
- **An aluminum pie plate**
- **One large candle, preferably with multiple wicks**

1. Make your "fog juice" by mixing a solution of one part glycerin to three parts distilled water. The "fog" is created when the solution is heated and starts to evaporate.

2. Cut the top off a two-liter soda bottle. Center the aluminum pie plate on the bottle spout and use tape to secure it.

3. Get some help lighting the candle and carefully place the bottle-plate contraption over it.

4. Add a teaspoon or so of fog juice. That should produce enough fog to fill a good-sized room. To replenish the fog, just pour additional teaspoons of fog juice into the fog machine as needed. Keep an eye on your device — never leave a lit candle unattended.

Create a Self-Carving Jack-o-Lantern

DIFFICULTY LEVEL

GET SOME HELP

STUFF YOU'LL NEED

- **A pumpkin**
- **A drill or a screwdriver**
- **A jar of peanut butter**

1. Draw your jack-o-lantern design on the pumpkin, then use the drill or screwdriver to poke holes along the lines of your design, almost like connect-the-dots.

2. Squish gobs of peanut butter into all of the holes.

3. Leave it outside and let the neighborhood squirrels gnaw away at its face. In a few days, you'll have a carved jack-o-lantern!

Make a Fantastical Beast Shadow Puppet

DIFFICULTY LEVEL

Artist Richela Fabian Morgan shares one of her favorite projects that lets your imagination run wild.

STUFF YOU'LL NEED

- **Scissors**
- **Thin cardboard or sturdy junk mail card mailers**
- **Brass fasteners or pipe cleaner**
- **Chopsticks or pencils**
- **Tape**
- **A lamp**

1 Think about an animal you'd like your beast to mimic: a tiger, a monkey, a dragon, anything.

2 Time to draw with scissors! The cool thing about shadow puppets is that little imperfections can create super-dramatic results. Without even sketching, start to cut out shapes for your beast's head and body (give it legs, wings, a tail or anything you want).

3 Poke holes in the body and the head where you want them to connect, then use the brass fasteners or pipe cleaners to attach them.

4 Tape the chopsticks or pencils to the back of the body and the head. Now you can make your beast begin to move.

5 Showtime! In a darkened room, you can cast a shadow of your beast on a wall using the lamp. Or see the next steps to build a simple shadow puppet theater.

MAKE A SHADOW PUPPET THEATER

STUFF YOU'LL NEED

- **A large cardboard box**
- **Scissors**
- **Large piece of white paper**
- **Tape**

1. Cut a rectangle on the front of the box.
2. Cut a big hole on the back of the box. This is where the lamp light will shine in.
3. Cut a hole in the side of the box big enough for you to get your hands and the puppet in.
4. From the inside, cover the front rectangle hole with a piece of white paper and tape it in place.
5. Darken the room, position a lamp behind the hole in the back of the box, then bring your beast into the side hole and let the story begin. Narrate your story and be sure to add lots of roaring!

DON'T TRY THIS AT HOME

RAT TRAP TOY CATAPULT

We're not making this up: Someone thought it'd be a good idea to make a toy out of something designed to squish rodents. Nasty!

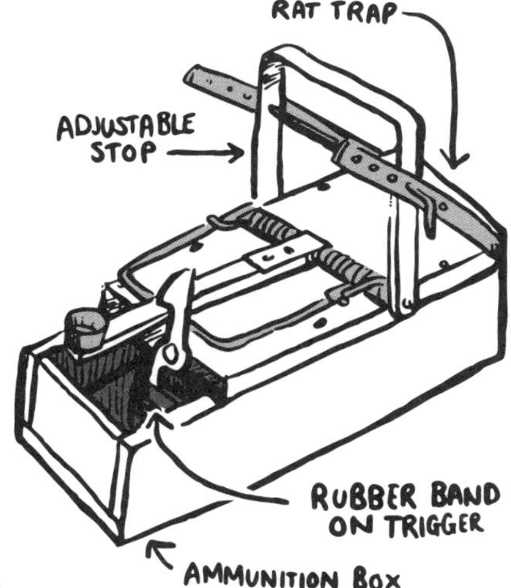

Get Started on Your ROCK STAR JOURNEY!

Singer and songwriter Mike Errico says a great way for future guitar gods and goddesses to begin making music is with the mighty ukulele!

WHAT IS A UKULELE?
A ukulele (pronounced yoo-kuh-lay-lee) looks like a small acoustic guitar, but it is much easier to play since it only has four strings (instead of six), and the strings are made of nylon instead of steel, which is much more comfortable on your fingertips.

HOW MUCH DO THEY COST?
Like any instrument, the price can vary a lot, but you can find a decent beginner one online or at a music store for around $30.

HOW DO I READ A CHORD CHART?
There are five simple chords to learn, and once you know those, you'll soon be able to play dozens of songs.

On a ukulele chord chart, the vertical lines are the strings and the horizontal lines are the fret bars that go across the neck of the ukulele. The strings, from left to right, are G, C, E and A. G is the thickest and lowest

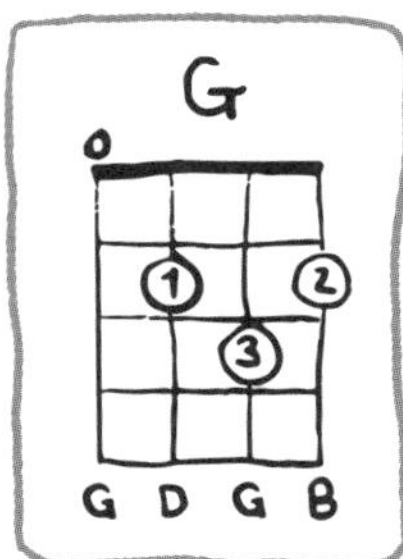

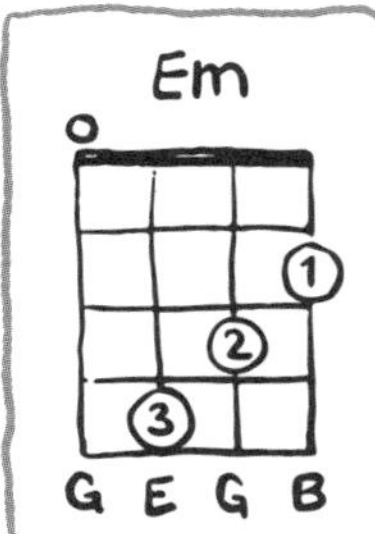

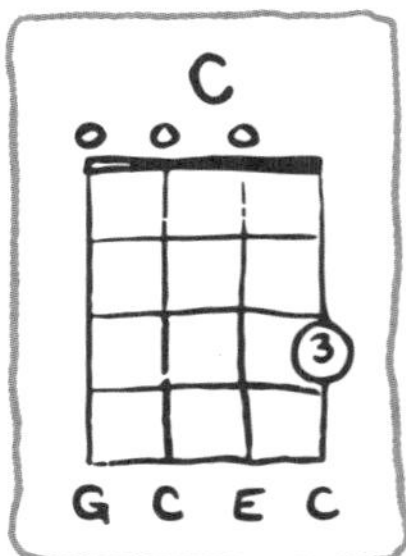

sounding string. They are often numbered on charts: 4 is the G, 3 is C, 2 is E and 1 is A.

The top line of the chart is the end of the ukulele neck. The next line down is the first fret, second fret, and so on.

The dots and numbers you see on the chart represent where you should press down on the fretboard, and which finger to use—1 is your index finger, 2 is your middle finger, 3 is your ring finger and 4 is your pinky.

Place your fingers in the positions on the chart and strum. Congrats, you're making music!

Practice each chord to get your hand comfortable, then practice switching between chords. It can be hard at first, but like riding a bike, once your fingers start to get the muscle memory of their positions, it gets easier.

HOW DO I TUNE MY UKULELE?

You can use a keyboard or even your phone to play a note and then gently twist the tuning knob until the sound matches. There are also lots of free tuning apps you can download.

HOW DO I LEARN SONGS?

There are tons of books and apps that have something called tabs, which write out songs with the basic chords and finger numbers, making them super-easy to play.

OKAY, NOW I CAN PLAY. WHAT'S NEXT?

Get creative! The fun thing, says Mike, is that once you know the basic chords, you can keep your hands in the same shape, and move that shape up and down the fretboard. You will hear all kinds of cool new sounds and maybe get inspired to write your own song!

"There's a reason why you see people like Taylor Swift smiling when they play music," says Mike. "It's really fun!"

PLAY HAPPY BIRTHDAY!

See the finger positions for each chord on the opposite page, then strum and sing along!

D **A**
Happy birthday to you

D **A**
Happy birthday to you

D **G**
Happy birthday dear **NAME**

D **A-D**
Happy birthday to you

START YOUR OWN YOUTUBE CHANNEL

DIFFICULTY LEVEL

Teen YouTube megastar Tiko (whose real name is Jayden) has over 6 million followers and makes more money than most adults do in a year. Here he tells you how he did it — and how you can too.

START BY HAVING FUN

"I started by making Fortnite montages, which are just little clips from the game with music over it. It was fun but wasn't getting a ton of views. Then I started using a voice changer that makes me sound like a little kid and that changed everything. I'll play Fortnite games where I get teamed up with strangers, and I say all of this weird stuff and get their reactions. I thought it was pretty funny, and I noticed that a lot of people liked it, so I switched over to that format and my following started to take off."

FIND YOUR OWN THING

"Experiment and try different stuff. You can go to Trending on YouTube gaming to see what is trending as a starting point, and then try to think of a way to put your own little spin on it."

HAVE A GOAL

"I started when I was in sixth grade. It took a little while to catch on. Honestly, I didn't think I'd ever get to 100,000 followers, but I just kept at it. And then the day I hit 100,000, I realized, wow, I can have fun and make money doing this."

DON'T RUSH

"Generally speaking, the more time you put into these videos, the better the quality. And higher quality videos tend to perform better. You can make something quick and just throw it out there, but the performance isn't great. I think that every video I do has the potential to go viral, so I try to put out the best stuff I can in a reasonable amount of time."

YOUTUBE IDEA FACTORY

SOME OF THE MOST COMMON TYPES OF VIDEOS ON YOUTUBE

TUTORIALS

Know how to do something really well? Make a series of videos showing off your expertise — anything from gaming to cooking to sports.

2

UNBOXING

Are you really into gadgets, toys or collectibles? Buy them and open them up on camera, narrating the entire process while sharing how excited you are.

GAMING

Like Tiko, use a software program that captures video of your screen and webcam (or just your audio). Be instructional or be a pest — just have fun!

YOU DON'T NEED FANCY EQUIPMENT
"I got to 100,000 followers just using my computer and a $40 microphone. The equipment does not really matter as long as you're putting out something that people enjoy."

BE CONSISTENT
"Posting regularly helps build your audience because they know to come back for more. I post every day, but you should do it at a pace that works for you."

AND TAKE BREAKS
"If it ever gets too much — like you are stressed about what to put out next, or your last few videos didn't do well — take a break. Take a day, week, month off if you need a mental health break. I always feel better and excited to start again when I come back from a trip."

HAVE FUN – REALLY!
"I would not be doing this if I was not enjoying it. I'm my own boss, so why would I make myself miserable?!"

HOW TO WRITE A SCARY STORY

Andrew Nance, author of horror and mystery books like *Daemon Hall* and *Odd Occurrences* explains how to tell a terrifying tale.

PUT YOUR EXTRAORDINARY STORY IN AN ORDINARY WORLD

"You want your reader to be able to imagine themselves standing in the shoes of your characters. It makes it scarier for them if it feels like this could really happen!"

GET TO THE GOOD STUFF FAST

"Don't keep your readers waiting; you want to get to the weird stuff quickly to grab their attention."

THINK ABOUT THE ENDING FIRST

"Twist endings are great for scary stories. Like just when your character thinks they're safe inside the house, they turn around and realize they've locked themselves inside the basement with the monster. Sometimes it is good to start with the idea of the ending — turns out Dad is really a vampire that has been terrorizing the town — and work your way back to get to that moment."

LOOK AT OLD MYTHS AND LEGENDS TO SPARK IDEAS

"There are a lot of ancient Greek myths, Native American legends and many other cultures that have characters you can get inspired by. Like Loki, the ancient god of mischief. You imagine him in the modern world and see what happens."

BASE YOUR CHARACTERS ON PEOPLE YOU KNOW

"It is easier to write realistic dialogue when you can base on things you've heard people say in real life. And you want to have a nice variety of characters, like a guy who is into music and a girl who is into sports and a super-smart kid who loves math. It makes it interesting to see these different kinds of characters come together and use their special talents to fight an evil monster."

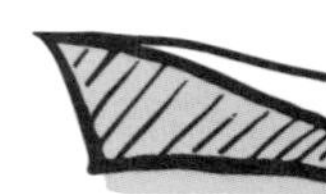

FIVE FREAKY READS

Here is a reading list for anyone who loves a good scare.

1. ***Coraline*** by Neil Gaiman

2. ***Fear Street series*** by R.L. Stine

3. ***Odd Occurrences*** by Andrew Nance

4. ***Scary Stories to Tell in the Dark*** by Alvin Schwartz

5. ***Something Wicked This Way Comes*** by Ray Bradbury

WRITE YOUR STORY — THEN FORGET IT.
"Revising is key to great writing. So after you are finished, put it away for a few days or a week, then go back and re-read it and see where you can make the sentences flow better."

PAY ATTENTION WHEN YOU ARE READING.
"A great thing to do when you are reading something you're enjoying, stop and ask yourself, 'Why am I scared now?' or 'Why am I laughing?' Re-read those pages and see what the writer did to make you feel a certain way."

ENTERTAINING PEOPLE IS FUN!
"There is nothing like getting a big reaction from your readers. I remember in grade school I brought in a scary story from an Alfred Hitchcock magazine. My teacher was reading it out loud and the bell rang, but no one in the class moved until she finished the story. That's when I knew I wanted to be a writer."

CHAPTER FIVE 5

FOR THE WIN

LET THE GAMES BEGIN!

This chapter is very competitive. It believes it is the best chapter in this book and it will, it will rock you! You're about to learn how to build your own games, how to get better at sports and beat everyone you play in Scrabble. See? It's the best! Is there a first-place trophy for book chapters?

Terms You Should Know

- **BREAKING BALL** A type of pitch in baseball where the ball doesn't move in a straight line. (p. 96)
- **CENTRIPETAL FORCE** A force that keeps things moving in a circular motion, pushing inward. (p. 116)
- **FOLLOW-THROUGH** Continuing your motion smoothly after you release a ball. (p. 97)
- **KINETICS** The science of motion. (p. 104)
- **SWEAT** That yucky stuff that drips down your face when you exercise a lot. (p. 105)
- **TRIATHLON** A race that combines swimming, biking, and running. (p. 104)

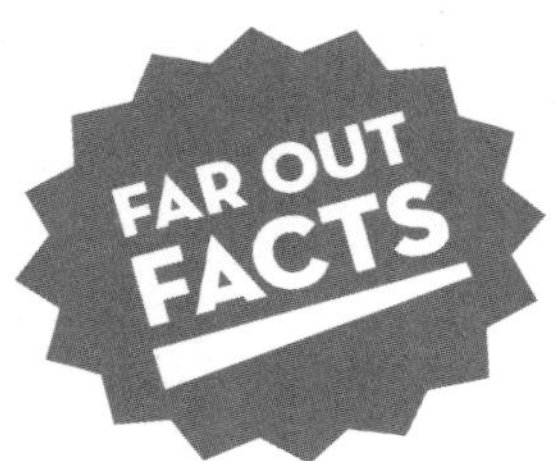

SUPER SPORTS TRIVIA

Put your knowledge of wacky sports facts to the test.

1. **What is the average lifespan of a baseball in Major League Baseball?**
   - A. 5 games
   - B. 7 innings
   - C. 6 pitches

2. **Why is a football nicknamed a "pigskin?"**
   - A. They look like piggies in the mud when they get dirty
   - B. The first balls were made with an inflated pig bladder
   - C. Tom Brady really loves bacon

3. **Babe Ruth used to do this to stay cool while playing games:**
   - A. Wore a cabbage leaf under his cap
   - B. Sat on an ice block in the dugout
   - C. Asked kids in the stands for a lick of their ice cream cones

4. **Which one of these sports was not an Olympic sport at one point?**
   - A. Tug of war
   - B. Bowling
   - C. Tag

5. **True or False: During World War II, so many players for the Pittsburgh Steelers and Philadelphia Eagles were in the service that they combined into one team called the Steagles.**
   - A. True
   - B. False

6. **Which sport do the most people in the world participate in?**
   - A. Baseball
   - B. Fishing
   - C. Bowling

7. Which sport did astronauts play on the moon in 1971?

A. Touch football
B. The high jump
C. Golf

8. Which of these “facts” about the original game of basketball is not true?

A. Players shot the ball into a peach basket, and the ref had to remove it after every score
B. Players were not allowed to dribble — they could only pass and shoot
C. Players had to be a minimum height of six feet to play

9. Why do fans at hockey games sometimes throw their hats onto the ice in unison?

A. They are annoyed by bad play from their team
B. Someone on the team scored three goals, called a “hat trick”
C. Whoever gets their hat closest to the center ice faceoff circle gets a free hotdog

10. Why has Rufus the Hawk, a real bird, become famous at the Wimbledon tennis tournament?

A. He once attacked Serena Williams
B. He grabbed a served ball out of the air
C. He scares away pigeons and keeps the courts clear of pigeon poop

SCORE

ROOKIE
Keep practicing; you’ll get better and better.

RISING STAR
Whoa, this kid could go pro!

7-10

WORLD CHAMPION
Get ready for your Gatorade bath!

ANSWER KEY **1.** C **2.** B **3.** A **4.** C **5.** A **6.** B **7.** C **8.** C **9.** B **10.** C

HOW TO THROW A CURVEBALL

MLB pitcher Corey Kluber tells you how.

GET A GRIP
"I hold my curveball almost the exact same way that I hold my fastball—with my index and middle fingers just along the narrow part of the seam."

CREATE SPIN
"With my fastball, I'm trying to keep my two fingers behind the ball as long as I can to pull down on it and create as much backspin as possible. With the curve, instead of trying to stay behind, it's almost the opposite. At the very end of the release, you try to get your hand in front of the ball to create that topspin, which makes it break. You're rolling your hand forward and down off the side of the ball as you snap your wrist."

TRY IT WITH A WIFFLE BALL
Do the same motions described above and keep the holes on the Wiffle Balls to the outside of your grip. Snap your wrist as you throw and watch that ball move like crazy as it nears the plate.

A curveball is a pitch that drops and moves to the side as it approaches home plate, making it tough to hit.

ON BOTH SIDES OF THE PLATE

HOW TO GET A GOOD HIT

Increase your chances of getting on base (or hitting a home run) with these pointers.

ELBOWS UP

You want to hold the bat over your back shoulder at about a 45-degree angle to the ground. Keep your back elbow up, parallel to the ground. This will help you have a level swing.

THINK ABOUT YOUR STANCE

Keep your feet about shoulder-width apart and have your knees slightly bent. Line yourself up with the plate by extending the bat and putting the sweet spot over the middle of the plate.

LOAD YOUR SWING

As you wait for the pitch, keep your bat up and shift your weight to your back foot.

STEP AND SWING

Keeping your eyes on the ball, take a step forward and shift your weight to the foot as you swing. Rotate your hips as you swing to get more power.

STAY LEVEL AND FOLLOW-THROUGH

Keep your swing level so you are not chopping down, which creates easy grounders, or swinging up, which results in pop-ups. And follow through to get your full power. Practice that swing on a tee as much as you can. Final tip: Work on your home run celebration high-five.

Shoot Three-Pointers Like an All-Star

You might not be tall enough to dunk yet, but with practice, you can become a lights-out three-point shooter.

YOUR POSITIONING
Point your toes at the rim and keep your feet about shoulder-width apart with your shooting side foot slightly forward. Square your shoulders to the rim (meaning that both of your shoulders should be directly facing it.)

YOUR LEGS
This is where the power for your shot comes from. Really put "the jump" in your jump shot as you shoot the ball.

YOUR HANDS
Hold the ball with the lines parallel to the floor. Put the index finger of your shooting hand on the air valve of the ball to find its center. Have some space between your palm and the ball.

EYES
Aim for the rim's net hooks that are nearest to you and think about dropping the ball just over them.

ARMS AND WRIST
When taking your shot, keep your elbow and wrist in line with each other. Push up as you jump and release the ball at a high point. Flick your wrist forward as you release and follow through with your hand facing down, so it looks like you are making a swan shape. Now, stick up three fingers as you run back to play defense.

Perfect Crossover Dribble

This trick is known as the "ankle breaker" because if done correctly, it leaves defenders tripping over themselves.

1. Practice dribbling with your right and left hand — you will need both to be able to do this move.

2. If you're starting with the ball in your right hand, step forward with your right foot and lean your body in that direction. Keep an eye on the defender's hips — if they turn in the direction that you're stepping, that means you've fooled them.

3. As the defender moves in that direction, shift back and bounce the ball to your other hand. (That's the "cross-over" part.) The defender will likely keep going in the wrong direction, while you shift and drive to the net in the other. If they try to shift back, there's a good chance they will fall. Now that you're open, take a shot, make a pass or dunk!

DID YOU KNOW?

LeBron James was a star wide receiver on his high school football team. But after he broke his wrist, he decided to stop playing football so that he could heal in time for his senior basketball season. Imagine if Tom Brady was throwing touchdown passes to LeBron? We wonder how high football scoreboards can go!

HOW TO THROW A PERFECT SPIRAL

Make more accurate passes and hit your receiver right in the numbers. Touchdown!

1. Grab the ball with your ring and pinky fingers in between the laces, and your thumb and index finger just below the white line (if your ball has it).

2. Hold the ball with your fingertip pads. There should be a little space between your palm and the ball.

3. Stand sideways with your feet shoulder-width apart. Put your weight back, then step forward as you release. Stay on the balls of your feet — throwing while flatfooted really zaps your power.

4. Your arm should move almost like you are making a chopping motion. Use your fingers to get the ball spinning in a spiral as you step forward and release it.

5. Make sure you follow through — your throwing hand thumb should wind up near your opposite thigh. Making a herky-jerky motion will make your pass wobbly.

WHY ARE SPIRALS BETTER?

As explained by physics experts at the Children's Museum in Indianapolis, the spinning helps fight the forces of gravity pulling the ball down and keeps it moving along its intended path. That makes it easier for a quarterback to aim and for a receiver to know where the ball is going — and for your team to win!

WHAT SIZE BALL SHOULD YOU USE?

It all depends on the size of your hands, but here is a guide to get your started.

SIZE 9 Official size for NFL, college, and players ages 14+

SIZE 8 Players ages 12-14

SIZES 6 AND 7 Pee-wee football and grade-schoolers

How to Aim in Pool

Nail your next shot.

1 Use your pool cue to make a line from the ball you want to sink to the pocket you want it to go. This is your "target line." Remember the exact spot where it starts on the ball.

2 Aim the cue ball for the target line spot on the ball you are trying to sink. This is the "aim line." Ready, aim, fire!

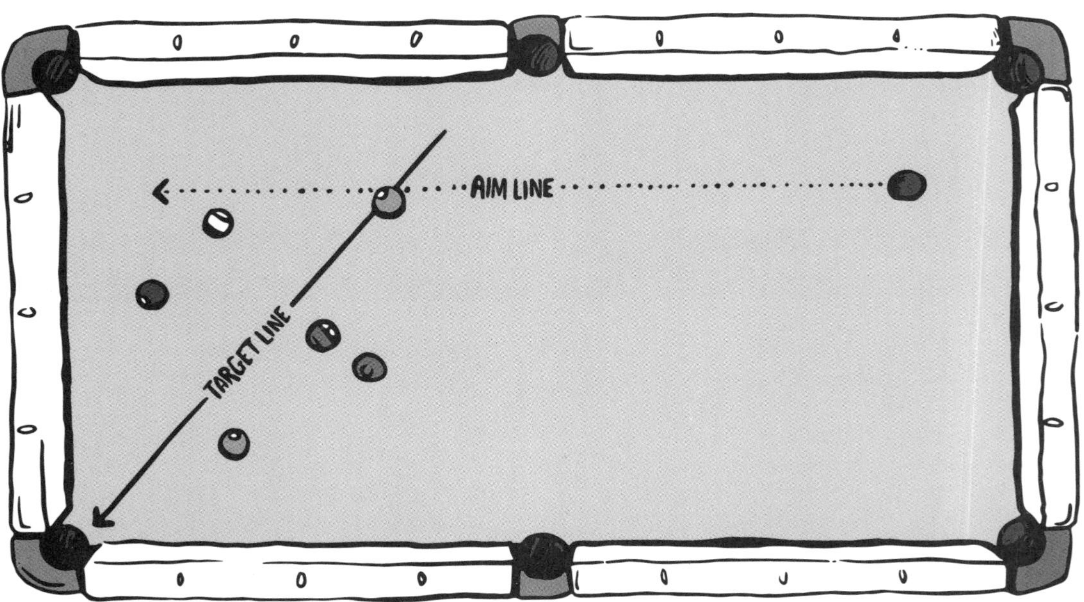

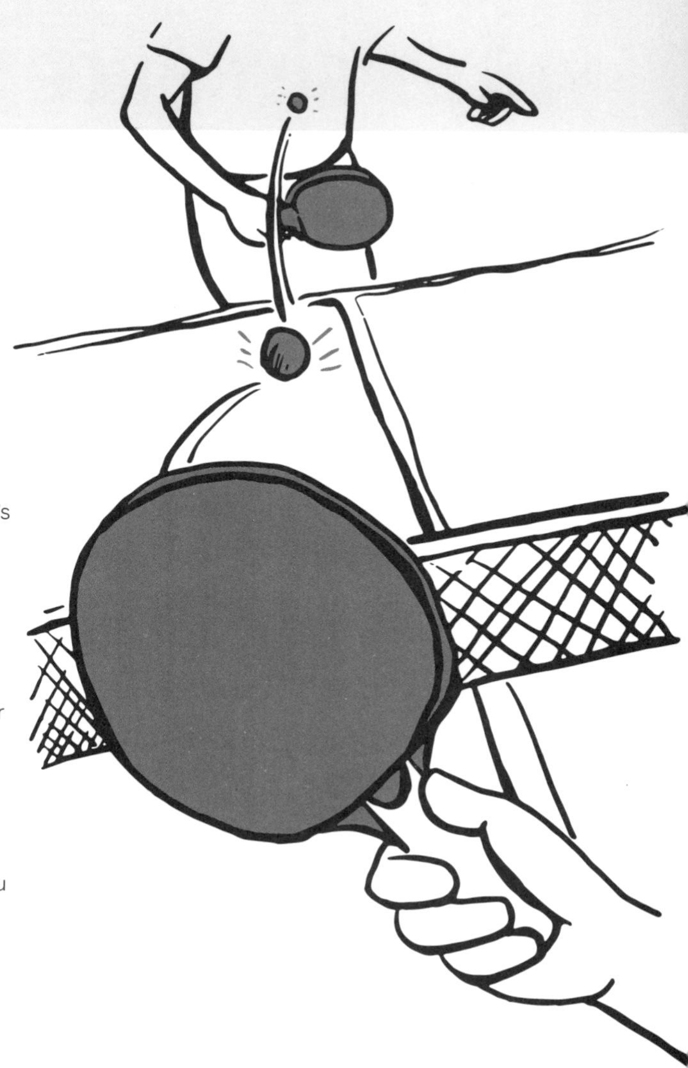

Get a Killer Shot in Ping-Pong

Make topspin your friend (and your opponent's worst enemy).

You hit a ball and off it goes. But did you know that a ball flying through the air is moving in two ways? There's straight velocity, the motion of the ball directly toward or away from you. And then there's spin — the ball rotating over itself. Spin causes the ball to do spooky, spectacular things, like ricochet off the table, over your opponent, and under a chair in the corner of the room.

Topspin is where the ball rotates over itself, bottom over top, as it's moving toward the other player. This causes the ball to speed up after it bounces on the table.

It's tough to return but easy to do. Here's how, according to Jim Butler, three-time U.S. men's singles table-tennis champion: Push up and over the ball as you hit it to create the spin. To make it extra hard to hit, try to aim it to bounce into the middle of your opponent's chest. Experts say that is the most difficult shot to return. (See how to make a floating ping-pong table on page 42!)

WHAT'S IT LIKE TO COMPETE IN ONE OF THE WEIRDEST RACES IN THE WORLD?

Writer James Vlahos explains his adventure competing in the cool and kooky Kinetic Grand Championship.

A 12-FOOT-LONG PICNIC BASKET. A giant silver lobster on wheels. Such are the sights you see at the Kinetic Grand Championship, a 50-mile, three-day long race over land, sand, water and mud that features some truly incredible works of art that move.

While it is amazing to look at for spectators, this annual event is not a parade; it is a contest. "Kinetics is about art, speed, and engineering," says Monica Topping, former president of the organization that puts on the race. "It's the triathlon of the art world."

The contest was started in 1969 by artists Hobart Brown and Jack Mays. The first race was won by a turtle that belched smoke and laid eggs. I came to the event to compete in a putrid-green, three-wheeled dune buggy called Visualize Whirled Peas, or VWP for short. Decorated with dangling tennis balls and spinning pinwheels, it has one tire up front and two in the back, and there's a similar configuration of seats for the trio of pilots to get situated.

VWP's inventor is Mike Ransom, who built the contraption from donated dirt track tires, abandoned bikes, and other dumpster-diving finds. Whether they are anti-car environmentalists or monster-truck fans, most racers, like Ransom, relish the challenge of turning trash into rolling treasure.

"How many bikes died to make that float?" a man on the street asks. "Probably about six or seven," Ransom says.

After our vehicle passes inspection (all vehicles must be certified as human-powered), we line up, and at noon a siren cuts through the air. Pedaling furiously and jockeying for position, Team VWP makes three laps around the square, then heads west out of town. The race is on.

As we pedaled, we passed a rickety white taco truck. Papier-mâché skeletons, one dressed as a bride and the other as a groom, sit in the front seats and grin toothily. "Newlydeads," reads the sign over their heads.

A couple of hours later, after driving down a long stretch of beach with waves sliding up beneath the tires, we turn inland and face a steep set of dunes. VWP makes it up the first one but stalls midway up the second. No matter how much we strain against the pedals, the machine won't move forward. The front wheel starts lifting up off the steep slope, and the whole contraption tilts dangerously backward. "Okay, that's it!" Ransom calls, signaling for everyone to jump off. "We're pushing."

After we reboard at the top of the hill, which is called Dead Man's Drop, a judge asks if we want to scout the steep descent on foot. "Nope, we'll be fine," Ransom replies as we wheel over the sandy lip. And he's right.

Our vehicle makes it across a mile-long section through Humboldt Bay, Styrofoam pontoons on each side of the craft keep us afloat. Paddle blades made from cut-up paint buckets and temporarily mounted on the wheels supply the propulsion.

At this point we realized we weren't going to come in first place. But in keeping with this crazy event, the ultimate prize at the race is not to come in first, but to come in exactly in the middle, which earns you the Medio-CAR Award. Sadly, we don't get that either, but our team is happy, especially Ransom, who is thrilled his machine stayed together. "Blood, sweat and gears," he says victoriously.

THE THRILLING THREE

REAL RACES FOR DIY-ERS

BARSTOOL RACES
Wisconsin

Racers speed down snow-covered slopes sitting on stools with skis attached to them.

POWER-TOOL DRAG RACES
Minnesota

Racers turn electric saws, angle grinders, and other tools into makeshift motors that power skateboards, scooters, bikes, and go-karts.

KRISPY KREME CHALLENGE
North Carolina

2400 calories, 12 donuts, five miles, one hour. Contestants run 2.5 miles to a Krispy Kreme, eat a dozen donuts, then run back 2.5 miles to the finish line.

ROLL A PERFECT HOOK SHOT

Rule your next bowling birthday bash.

Mike Fagan, a winner of the Professional Bowlers Association World Championship, explains how to roll a bowl so it hits the sweet spot between the first and second row of pins to get a strike.

1

Start your swing.

Start your swing, letting the weight of the ball carry your arm backward.

Don't rush.

Don't rush. Use the momentary pause at the top of your backswing to make sure your hand is positioned underneath and to the inside of the ball as much as possible. This allows for maximum rotation.

Create spin.

As you release the ball, you want to rotate your wrist, not your elbow, to create spin. Your hand should follow all the way through the outside of the ball and be almost vertical on the follow-through.

Practice.

As you get better, you can try rotating your wrist faster, which increases revolutions and power.

THROW A BULLSEYE

LEARN THESE DARTBOARD POINTERS

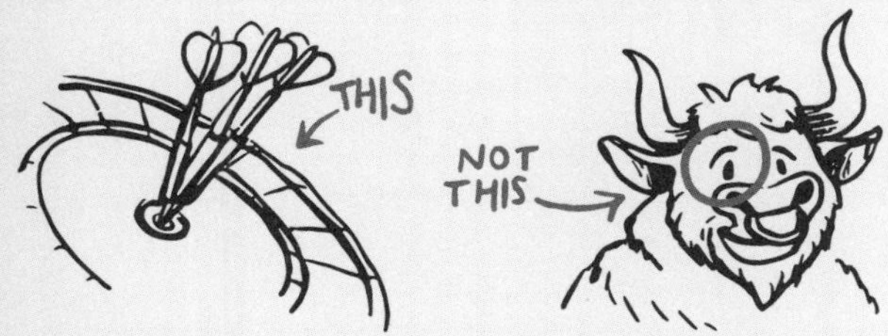

- Darts are like really sharp, slow-moving bullets: Their path arches up and then down.
- The harder you throw, the straighter the dart will fly, but you'll have less control.
- Point the toe of your throwing side toward the board and open your other leg to the side.
- Limit your movement to the elbow and wrist. Extend your arm about three-quarters of the way and release the dart.
- Follow through until your finger is pointing at the board.
- To keep a shot straight, find the dart's center of gravity and balance it on your thumb, letting your fingers gently hold it in place.
- Unless you're playing some weird game, always aim for the triple 20. It's worth 10 points more than the bull's-eye, and it's bigger.

DON'T TRY THIS AT HOME

FROM THE BAD IDEA FILES

A DINING ROOM CHAIR SLED

Here's another wacky (but true) project from the *Popular Mechanics* archives: If riding on this contraption doesn't result in you getting injured, taking your family's furniture into the snow will definitely result in you getting grounded!

Make a Basketball Catapult Game

DIFFICULTY LEVEL

Play one–on-one basketball no matter what the weather is like outside.

STUFF YOU'LL NEED

- 1" x 6" x 12" white pine board
- ⅜" x 48" round wood dowel
- Wire coat hanger
- 2" pan-head wood screws
- Optix 0.08" x 8" x 10" clear acrylic sheet
- Nerf Rival refill-pack foam balls
- 10 golf tees (two colors)
- Sandpaper

1. Cut the 1- x 6- x 12-inch board into lengths of 4 ½ inches, 4 inches, and 1 ½ inches. Knock off any rough edges with sandpaper.

2. The 4 ½-inch section forms the base. Two inches in from one of the cut sides, drill a ⅜-inch hole in the center to hold the post. Use a tape measure and a pencil to lightly draw two parallel lines one inch in from the finished sides. Starting an inch from the front of the base, mark off five ½-inch increments on each line for the scoring tees. Drill holes at those marks with a 3⁄16-inch bit, then erase the line.

3. The four-inch section will be the backboard. On one of the cut edges, drill a hole in the center with a ⅜-inch bit for the post. On the face of the backboard, measure up ½ inch from the bottom and drill two holes, one inch apart and centered over the post, with a 1⁄16-inch bit.

4. Use a saw to cut the dowel to length (see diagram). Spread some glue on its ends and insert one end in the base and the other in the backboard. Align the backboard so its face is parallel with the front edge of the base.

5 Cut a piece of wire coat hanger to about five inches. Bend the wire so it forms a circle. Grip each end with pliers to make a 90-degree bend. Insert the ends into the holes you drilled in the backboard.

6 Use a marker to indicate the cut line on the acrylic sheet (see diagram) and cut the catapult arm to size using a jigsaw and a fine cutting blade.

7 Mark the location of the basketball holder on the acrylic according to the diagram, then bore the hole using a ¾-inch spade bit. Drill slowly to avoid cracking the plastic. Use a ¼-inch drill bit to bore the pilot holes for the mounting screws through the other end of the acrylic and into the wedge.

8 The remaining scrap of pine will form the wedge. With one corner as your starting point, measure one inch along one side and three inches along the other. Mark both points and cut a straight line between them with the jigsaw. Apply a drop of glue to the wedge's back and glue it to the 1½-inch block from step 1. Fasten the catapult to the wedge with two screws.

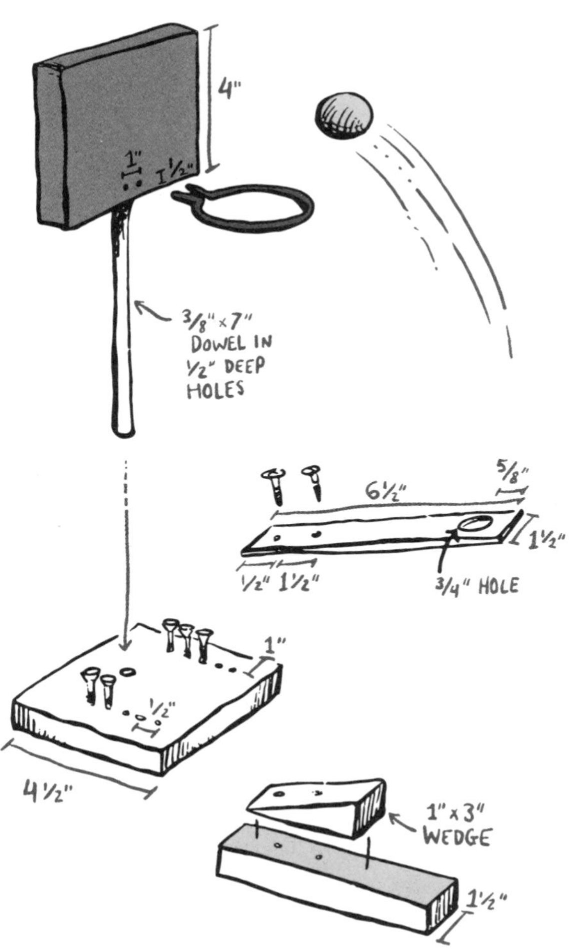

RULES

Competitors take turns shooting from a set distance. (You can vary where you shoot from for each shot to keep things interesting.) Take a golf tee for every shot you make. The person with the most tees is declared the new King!

See cool card tricks on p. 52

SUPER-FUN CARD GAMES

The rules to three simple and totally fun games to play (and win, of course).

Crazy Eights

PLAYERS NEEDED
Two or more

THE GOAL
Get rid of all your cards first!

1. Every player gets dealt five cards, face down.
2. The rest of the deck goes into the middle, and the first card at the top of the deck gets flipped over. (If you draw an eight, place it back into the middle of the deck and flip another card.)
3. Starting to the dealer's left, each player tries to get rid of a card by placing it face up on top of the flipped over card. It must match either the card's suit (heart, diamond, spade or club) or the card's denomination (its number, type of face card or ace).
4. All eights are wild, meaning it can be used to cover any card. After placing it, the player declares what suit it is, and the next player has to match it.
5. Keep going around until a player can't match a card. That player then takes cards from the top of the pile until they get one they can play.
6. If the pile runs out, the player must pass to the next player to the left. Then, keep the left card facing up, and shuffle the rest and turn it over face down for a new pile.
7. The first player to get rid of all their cards wins!

HOW TO SHUFFLE A DECK

Instructions from the makers of Bicycle playing cards.

1. Half the deck into two neat piles that are roughly the same size.
2. Position them side by side with the long side facing you.
3. Put your thumbs on the two inside corners at the top of each deck, and your index fingers on the opposite corners. Your other fingers can help keep the piles in place.
4. Use your thumbs to push the top corners up, push the two halves toward each other, then let the cards fall. The corners of the decks should be shuffled.
5. Push the connected piles into one, then repeat a few times to ensure a good mix.

Go Fish

PLAYERS NEEDED
2-5

THE GOAL
Get the most "books" of cards, which are four-of-a-kind

1. For two or three players, the dealer deals out seven cards to everyone. For four or five, each gets five cards. The pack is placed face down in the middle.
2. The player to the left of the dealer starts. They look at their hand and decide which they want to try to get four of. For example, you might have already have two 10s, so that seems easier.
3. Time to fish! They choose any other player and say, "Give me your 10s." Note: The fisher must have at least one of the cards they are asking for.
4. The player who is asked for the cards must hand over all the cards the fisher asked for. (If they asked for kings and you have three of them, you hand them all over.) Getting a match is called a "catch."
5. If the fisher makes a catch, they get to go again and can ask the same player or a different one for a card. They keep going as long as they are making catches. If the asked player doesn't have what the fisher wants, they say, "Go fish!"
6. The fisher then takes a card from the top of the pile in the middle, and the next player goes. When a player gets four of a kind (like four Jacks, four 10s, etc.) that is called a book. They place them on the table face up and go again.
7. If a player runs out of cards, they can pick from the middle pile and fish for a matching card. If there are no cards left in the middle, the player is out. The game ends when all thirteen books are made. The winner is the player with the most books.

Acey Deucy

PLAYERS NEEDED
Two (but preferably more)

THE GOAL
Correctly guess a card's ranking

1. Players get pretzels or something fun to bet with. Each player puts five pieces in the middle. This collective pile is called the pot.
2. The first player is dealt two cards face up then bets anywhere from nothing to the amount in the pot that the third card they are dealt will fall in between the two cards they have. For example, if you have a three and a 10, you are betting that the next card will be anything from four to nine. So an Ace and a two (called a deuce) is your strongest hand.
3. If the third card does fall in between, the player takes what they bet out of the pot.
4. If the third card is outside the two cards, they add the amount they bet to the pot. If not, you have to put double what you bet into the pot.
5. If the pot is won, all players "ante up" (meaning, they put in a fresh batch of whatever you are betting), and you play on until you don't want to bet and would prefer eating your winnings!

Make a Cornhole Set Out of a Single Piece of Plywood

DIFFICULTY LEVEL

GET SOME HELP

Fun to build, even more fun to play!

STUFF YOU'LL NEED

- **1 sheet of ¾" sanded plywood**
- **18 1½" No. 6 wood screws**
- **Drill**
- **A compass**
- **Pencil**
- **Sandpaper**
- **Cornhole bags**

1. Cut the plywood into four 24-inch x 48-inch sheets.

2. On one quarter-sheet, mark a spot nine inches down from the top and 12 inches in from one side. Use a compass to draw a six-inch-diameter circle around the point. Drill a starter hole just inside the circle, then use a jigsaw to cut out the hole. Repeat on another quarter-sheet. Smooth the inside edges of the holes with sandpaper.

3. Cut a 12 ¾-inch length from one of the remaining two quarter-sheets. Measure 1 ½ inches in on the top and 11 ¼ inches in on the bottom and draw a diagonal line between the two points. Cut along this line, then cut 1 ⁹⁄₁₆ inches off of the short end of the triangles you just made.

4. Crosscut the remaining 11 ¼ by 48–inch piece of plywood into two 22 ½-inch lengths, then rip one down to a width of 1 ¼ inches. These pieces form the front and back of the base.

5 Shave down the tops of the front and back pieces to approximately match the slope of the triangles.

 Assemble the pieces and screw together (making sure the heads of the screws are sunk and not sticking out where they can snag the bag). Who wants to play first?

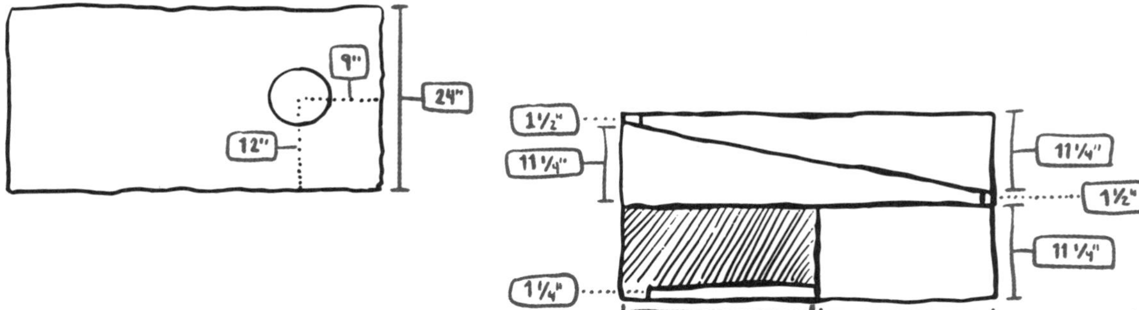

THE RULES OF CORNHOLE

Set up the two boards 21 feet from each other. Two players, one from each team, stand at each board. (You can also play with just two players and go back and forth.)

The two players begin with four bean bags and alternate tosses to the opposite board. A bag that goes in the hole is worth three points. If it stays on the board, it is worth one point.

Teams' scores cancel each other out. So if you score seven and your opponent gets four, you get three points for that round.

The first team to 21 wins.

Make a Giant Jenga Tower

DIFFICULTY LEVEL

All you need is wood, a saw, and some stacking ability.

STUFF YOU'LL NEED

- Eight 96" 2 x 4s
- Sandpaper

1. Measure and cut nine 10 ½" sections on each 2 x 4.

2. Sandpaper off the rough edges.

3. Stack them up in the Jenga configuration. Three blocks make one level, then the next level's blocks should be set rotated 90-degrees, and so on. (This will give you 24 levels. Store-bought Jenga games have 18.)

4. Time to play! The winner is the last player to remove and stack a block on top of the tower before it collapses.

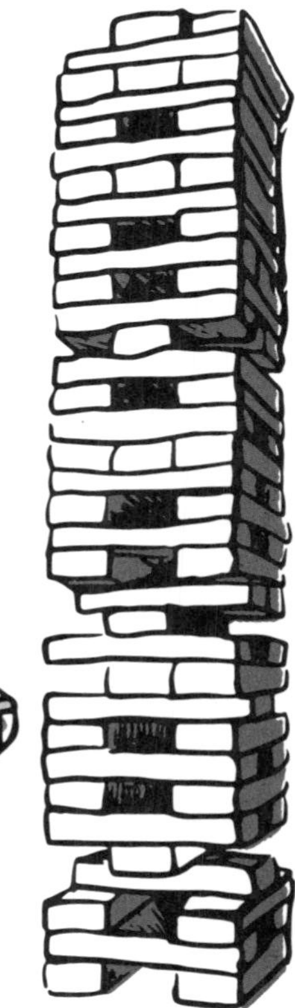

Be a Scrabble Master

Top tips from professional Scrabble Players. (Yes, that's a real thing.)

THE POWER OF TWO

Acquaint yourself with the over 100 two-letter words that are acceptable. These include AA, AB, EW, AH, XI, XU, YA, and ZA. (The great part is you don't have to know what they mean!)

HUNT FOR OPPORTUNITIES

We tend to focus on words on the board that we put down but look to ones your opponent played and look for chances to build on them. Add an S to the end of their CAR and you just scored easy points.

HAVE BOARD VISION

Pros don't just think about where they can make words on the board — they make sure that they aren't creating an easy opportunity for their opponent to use a double or triple letter square.

THINK ABOUT YOUR LEFTOVERS

Putting out a great big word with lots of points is sweet, but it can put you in a jam for your next turn if you use up all of your vowels and only have hard-to-use letters like W and V.

DON'T FEAR THE Q

Try to memorize a bunch of Q words so you don't get stuck. "quadi," "qaid," and "faqir" are just a few.

BIG WORDS, BIG SCORES

SOME LEGAL (AND TOTALLY WEIRD) PLAYABLE WORDS AND THEIR MEANINGS

HAECCEITY
The essence of individuality.

SYZYGY
The perfect alignment of three celestial bodies.

TSUTSUGAMUSHI
A type of bacteria.

BRRR
The sound you make when you are cold.

CRWTHS
An ancient musical instrument.

THE SCIENCE OF GETTING BIG AIR IN THE HALF-PIPE

Olympic gold medal winner Kelly Clark explains how she gets way, way, way up there.

1. APPROACH

In the pipe, riders can travel up to 40 mph, but they have to fight the forces that sap speed. As Clark transitions from flat bottom to vertical wall, centripetal force pushes her down. She pumps her legs, which stiffens her body and causes her to exert more force on the ground. According to Newton's third law of motion, that force pushes back and boosts her speed.

2. LAUNCH AND FLIGHT

If snowboarders jumped like basketball players, they'd fly away from the wall and toward the center of the pipe, instead of up above the lip. Clark generates height by rotating her body as she reaches the lip to create vertical velocity. Once in the air, she pulls her arms close to her body to increase rotation and spin. "The more compact I am," she says, "the faster I spin."

3. LANDING

Clark spots her landing two-thirds through a trick. When landing, she must "'pull the chute'—you make yourself as big as you can to slow your rotation," she says. To maintain speed into the next trick, she reenters the pipe as high on the wall as possible. When she lands, Clark must keep her body rigid; flexing her knees would absorb energy and zap her speed.

DID YOU KNOW?

At the Beijing 2022 Olympic Winter Games, Japanese snowboarder Kaishu Hirano didn't get a medal, but he did set a record for the biggest air in snowboarding. During his final run, he soared 24 feet and 4 inches above the half pipe!

MAD
SCIENCE
O
H
Ne
N
He
Na

MWAHAHAHA!

Grab a white lab coat and practice your best maniacal laugh — by the end of this chapter, you will be a certified mad scientist. (Or a happy scientist, depending on what kind of mood you're in.) We're going to be looking up at black holes millions of light-years away and down at dinosaur fossils millions of years old. We'll be performing mind-bending physics experiments and peering inside a 200-foot-tall, fire-breathing lizard. If all that sounds a little freaky, don't worry, we're also going to make a pretty sweet paper airplane. Because, hey, even hardworking mad scientists like you need to have fun sometimes.

Terms You Should Know

- **ANTIBIOTIC** Medicine that fights infections caused by bacteria. (p. 120)
- **ELEMENT** A pure substance. (p. 120)
- **EON** A unit of time equal to about one billion years. (p. 127)
- **EXOPLANETS** Planets that orbit stars other than our Sun. (p. 135)
- **HUBBLE TELESCOPE** A space telescope that orbits the Earth. (p. 129)
- **METER** A metric unit of length, equal to about three feet. (p. 123)
- **NOBEL PRIZE** A very prestigious prize given to people whose work helps humanity. (p. 120)
- **POTENTIAL ENERGY** Energy that is stored in an object. (p. 125)
- **RADIOACTIVE** Material that decays, releasing energy that is harmful to living things. (p. 120)
- **WORLD DOMINATION** That's the goal of every mad scientist, right?

TOTALLY TRUE, SUPER-WEIRD AND SOMETIMES GROSS SCIENCE FACTS

FAR OUT FACTS

Ewww! GROSS!

You won't forget these tidbits, no matter how hard you try!

1 The average cumulus cloud (the big puffy cotton ball-looking ones) weighs about 1 million pounds.

2 Researchers learned that rats laugh when they get tickled.

3 The atmospheres in Neptune, Uranus and Saturn are truly bizarre — scientists believe that the conditions cause it to rain diamonds.

4 Marie Curie won the Nobel Prize for discovering and studying radium, a radioactive element. Her notebooks were so contaminated with radium that they are kept in lead-lined boxes to prevent them from making people sick.

5 If you want to see a living dinosaur, just look up in a tree. Birds are dinosaurs and are classified in the same group as a T. Rex!

6 You can't burp in space. Gravity is required to separate gas, liquids and solid food in our tummies.

7 Penicillin, the first antibiotic drug, was discovered after a scientist left a mess in his lab. After returning from summer vacation,

Dr. Alexander Fleming found mold — and it was killing harmful bacteria he was studying. Who knows, your messy room could lead to a scientific breakthrough!

8 On average, a person walks the equivalent of five times around the world over the course of their lifetime — that's 124,505 miles!

9 A blood cell takes about 60 seconds to make a roundtrip around your body back to your heart.

10 Bad morning breath happens because your mouth dries out when you sleep, and a lack of saliva allows more smelly bacteria to multiply. Get out that toothbrush!

11 Your nose produces about 30 cups of snot a week.

12 Farts exit the body at seven miles per hour. (Whose job was it to measure that?)

13 You shed the entire outer layer of your skin every two to four weeks. (A rattlesnake sheds its skin three to four times a year.)

14 Close the lid before you flush — germs can spray as far as six feet away!

15 If you aren't afraid of tarantulas yet, this might help: They inject their prey with a poison that turns their insides into a liquid that the spider then drinks.

16 Lobsters pee out of their faces.

17 Cockroaches can live for a week after their head gets cut off.

18 A year is the amount of time it takes the Earth to make a full revolution around the sun. If you are 12 years old here on Earth, you'd be only 6 on Mars because it takes about twice as long for Mars to make the trip.

19 Dragonflies can see in every direction at once. Good luck sneaking up on one!

20 Astronauts stretch up to three inches taller in outer space due to the lack of gravity.

Incredible Center of Gravity Experiment

DIFFICULTY LEVEL

Be amazed by the physics concept of changing the center of gravity.

STUFF YOU'LL NEED

- **String**
- **A filled water bottle**
- **3 toothpicks**
- **Something heavy** (like a stack of books and a milk jug)

1. Tie the string around the water bottle opening and create a loop about a foot or two long.
2. Place a toothpick on the edge of a table, partly sticking out. Place the heavy object on the end.
3. Hang the water bottle from the toothpick.
4. Use one toothpick to form a little bridge with the string loop.
5. Take the third toothpick and connect the edge of the table toothpick to the bridge toothpick.
6. Remove the heavy object and see that the bottle remains hanging!

WHAT'S GOING ON?

By constructing the bridge, you change the center of gravity from being over the table to being even with the table. That's a little hard to understand, so just say this if anyone asks how you did it: magic!

Measure the Speed of Light With Chocolate

A science experiment with yummy results.

DIFFICULTY LEVEL

STUFF YOU'LL NEED

- **A full-size chocolate bar** (Hershey's works great)
- **A microwave oven**
- **A calculator**
- **A ruler**

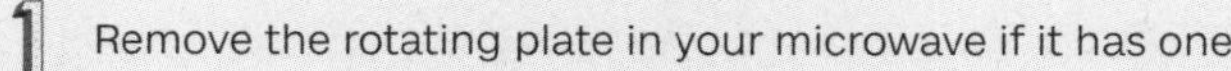

1 Remove the rotating plate in your microwave if it has one.

2 Put the chocolate bar on a paper plate with the smooth side facing up.

3 Microwave it on high for about 15 seconds, until you start to see two melted spots forming.

4 Measure the distance between the closest edges of the melted spots in centimeters. This distance shows where the light wave went in and came out of the chocolate. That number equals half a microwave wavelength.

5 Use your calculator to divide that number by 100. This gives you the distance in meters. Multiply that number by two to get the full wavelength distance.

6 Look inside the door of your microwave (or behind it) to find a sticker that has information about the machine. Look for the frequency number. Most will have a frequency of 2450 MHz, which equals 2,450,000,000 waves per second.

7 Multiply the wavelength distance number you got in step 5 by the frequency number in step 6. You get a number close to 300,000,000? Well, 299,792,458 meters/second is the speed of light! Now it's time to figure out how to turn your microwave into a time machine. (Or to eat your experiment.)

A SPEEDY HISTORY OF ROLLER COASTERS

Harnessing the laws of physics has never been more fun.

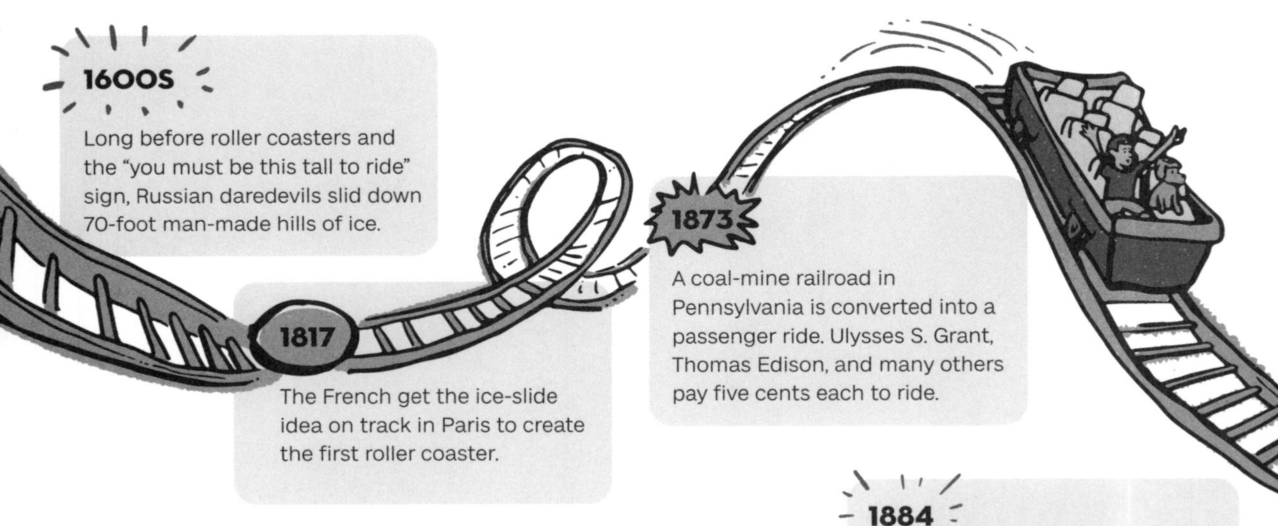

1600S

Long before roller coasters and the "you must be this tall to ride" sign, Russian daredevils slid down 70-foot man-made hills of ice.

1817

The French get the ice-slide idea on track in Paris to create the first roller coaster.

1873

A coal-mine railroad in Pennsylvania is converted into a passenger ride. Ulysses S. Grant, Thomas Edison, and many others pay five cents each to ride.

1884

U.S. inventor LaMarcus Adna Thompson designs the first Coney Island coaster in Brooklyn, NY; Switchback Railway involves coasting down 600 feet of wooden track at a breathtaking six mph.

1927

The 2640-foot Coney Island Cyclone causes a sensation when it opens with speeds of 60 mph and an 85-foot plunge. (It is still in operation today!)

1959

Disneyland's Matterhorn in Anaheim, California is the first tubular-steel-track roller coaster in the world.

DID YOU KNOW?

Roller coasters don't have engines because they rely on gravity to propel them. As a coaster is pulled up a hill, its potential energy increases. Then that energy is released as kinetic energy as the coaster makes it over the hill and gravity takes over (and you start screaming your head off).

1992

Design firm Bolliger & Mabillard builds the first inverted coaster, Batman: The Ride, for Six Flags Great America in Illinois. Cars run on the underside of the tracks, with riders' legs dangling.

2010

Ferrari World in Abu Dhabi unveils Formula Rossa; it goes from 0 to 150 mph in 4.9 seconds, the fastest in the world.

2013

Six Flags Magic Mountain in California unveils plans for Full Throttle, a roller coaster with the tallest loop in the world—160 feet in the sky.

2022

SeaWorld Orlando opens the Ice Breaker roller coaster. The ride features a reverse launch that flies along a 93-foot-tall spike with a 100-degree angle, the steepest vertical drop in Florida.

BIG TIME BUILD

BUILD AN AIR PUMP WATER BOTTLE ROCKET

DIFFICULTY LEVEL

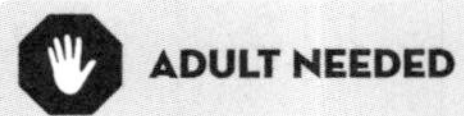

Get pumped up for this high-flying vehicle.

STUFF YOU'LL NEED

- **Electric drill with ¹⁄₁₆", ⁵⁄₃₂", and ¼" bits**
- **One No. 4 size rubber stopper** (1" long, 1" diameter at the fat end)
- **One 8" length of ³⁄₁₆"** (outside diameter) **copper tubing**
- **Bicycle pump with inflation needle**
- **Heavy card stock**
- **One two-liter plastic bottle**
- **Duct tape**
- **One drinking straw**
- **Four 1" square wood blocks**
- **One ½" plywood board, 12" to 16" square**
- **One ¼" threaded steel rod, 18" long**
- **Four ¼" nuts**
- **Two washers, ¼" hole, 1" diameter**

MAKE THE STOPPER ASSEMBLY

1. Drill a ¹⁄₁₆-inch hole through the middle of the stopper.
2. Widen the hole by drilling the ⁵⁄₃₂-inch bit about ½ inch into the top (wider part) of the stopper.
3. Insert the copper tubing into the ⁵⁄₃₂-inch hole.
4. Push the inflation needle into the hole in the bottom of the stopper so that it feeds into the copper tube.

BUILD THE ROCKET

1. Make fins from card stock; attach to the bottle with duct tape.
2. Tape the eight-inch drinking straw to the side of the bottle (oriented from top to bottom).

BUILD THE LAUNCHPAD

1. Attach square blocks to the corners of the launch platform (plywood), using quick-setting glue or 1¼-inch wood screws.
2. Place the rocket in the center of the launch platform and mark the spot directly below the plastic straw.
3. Drill a ¼-inch hole through the mark; insert the steel rod into the hole and fix in place with nuts and washers.
4. Prepare the hydro-pump rocket for launch.
5. Attach the bicycle pump to the inflation needle.
6. Fill the bottle one-third full with water, below the top of the copper tube.
7. Push the stopper assembly firmly into the bottle's mouth.
8. Invert the rocket and slide the soda straw onto the rod.

TIME FOR LAUNCH!

1. Pump air into the rocket. The amount of pressure required to fire the rocket will vary, depending on how clean the seal between the rubber stopper and the rocket is and how firmly the stopper is placed.
2. After several pumps, the pressure inside the rocket will be great enough to overcome the friction holding the stopper in place. Now comes the cool part as the stopper releases from the rocket. The rocket launches high into the air, shooting a trail of water behind it. Zoom!

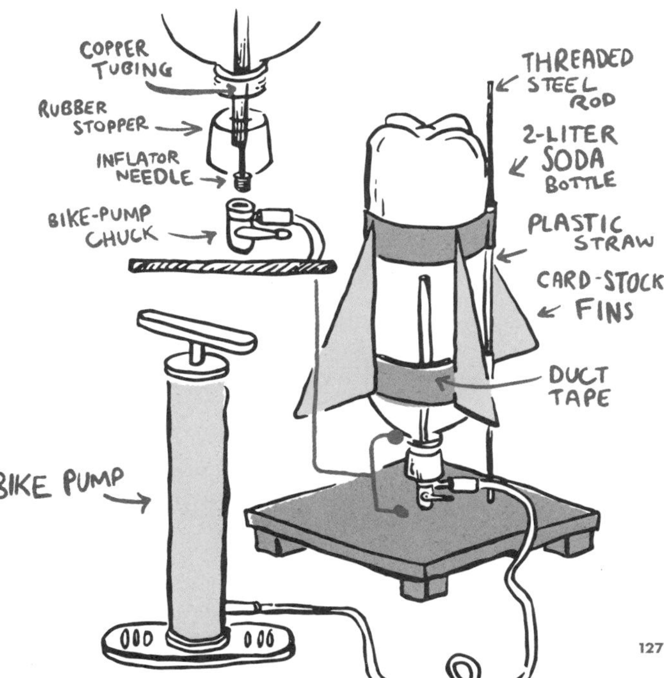

REAL LIFE ADVENTURE

LET'S GO STROLLING IN OUTER SPACE

A history of spacewalks. *(Do not read if you are afraid of heights!)*

March 18, 1965
ALEXEI LEONOV'S FIRST SPACE WALK
Alexei Leonov became the first man to perform an EVA (extra-vehicular activity) in space, exiting his Voskhod 2 capsule for 12 minutes. The vacuum of space caused Leonov's spacesuit to inflate more than was anticipated. He had to force air out of his spacesuit to re-enter the airlock of the craft.

June 3, 1965
EDWARD WHITE BECOMES THE FIRST AMERICAN SPACEWALKER
Astronaut Edward White, who took America's first spacewalk, described ending his 36-minute spacewalk and going back into the Gemini 4 spacecraft as the "saddest moment of my life."

November 12-14, 1966
BUZZ ALDRIN ON THE GEMINI 12
Buzz Aldrin spent three days in 1966 making spacewalks, the longest at 2 hours and 18 minutes, during which he installed a series of cameras on the craft. The next day, he completed the first successful complex spacewalk and proved a number of technologies to be used in the Apollo missions.

January 16, 1969
FIRST TWO-PERSON SPACEWALK
Yevgeni Khrunov and Aleksei Yeliseyev became the team behind the first two-person EVA when the Soyuz 4 docked with the Soyuz 5 capsule. The two transferred between modules to ensure a successful docking.

July 20, 1969
HUMANS WALK ON THE MOON
Neil Armstrong and Aldrin became the first men to walk on the moon after landing on the surface during the Apollo 11 mission. The descent of the Eagle hit trouble when the craft almost ran out of fuel, but the two landed, marking the first of five moon visits and making history.

May 25, 1973
SKYLAB REPAIRS
To get America's first space station to work correctly in space, astronaut Paul Weitz made a spacewalk to repair the solar array (a collection of solar panels) so it could deploy properly, saving the mission and marking the first space station EVA.

April 7, 1983
FIRST SPACE SHUTTLE EVA
Story Musgrave and Donald Peterson were the first astronauts to perform an EVA from the new Space Shuttle program during mission STS-6, where they performed tests in the cargo bay of the Challenger.

February 7, 1984
FIRST UNTETHERED SPACEWALK
Using a pack called the Manned Maneuvering Unit, astronaut Bruce McCandless became the first spacewalker to float freely, unconnected to a spacecraft.

July 25, 1984
FIRST WOMAN TO WALK IN SPACE
Russian cosmonaut Svetlana Savitskaya becomes the first woman to successfully perform an EVA during 1984's Salyut 7 VE-4 mission. NASA astronaut Kathryn Sullivan performed an EVA in October 1984, becoming the first American woman to do so.

December 6-9, 1993
FIRST HUBBLE SERVICING
The Hubble Space Telescope is located 347 miles above the Earth. That's low Earth orbit, but it's far from most shuttle missions. (The ISS orbits 249 miles above the Earth.) Repairing Hubble was risky, but a series of four EVAs over the course of four days in 1993 corrected imaging problems with the telescope and enabled the breathtaking views we've seen over the last two decades.

October 18, 2019
FIRST ALL-WOMAN TEAM IN SPACE
Astronauts Christina Koch and Jessica Meir's spacewalk outside the International Space Station makes history as the first female team.

DID YOU KNOW?

In America, we call them "astronauts." In Russia, they are called "cosmonauts." In China, they're known as "taikonauts."

AMERICAN ROCKET HALL OF FAME

Name	**SCOUT A**	**SATURN V**	**SPACE SHUTTLE**	**ATLAS V 551**	**DELTA IV HEAVY**	**FALCON**
Launch	1960	1967	1981	2003	2004	2018
Height	76 ft	363 ft	184.5 ft	204 ft	232 ft	230 ft
Weight	48,600 lb	6.2 million lb	4.5 million lb	1.2 million lb	1.6 million lb	3.1 million lb
Payload	Department of Defense and research satellites	Apollo astronauts	Astronauts, Hubble Space Telescope	Juno, New Horizons spacecrafts	Orion spacecraft, classified satellites	Elon Musk's Tesla Roadster

LET'S GO FIND SOME FOSSILS

Dinosaur expert "Dino" Don Lessem worked on *Jurassic Park* and builds incredible life-sized robot dinosaurs for museums. He has also hunted for fossils all around the world. Here are his tips for finding one of your own.

YOU HAVE A PRETTY GOOD CHANCE

"Eight out of 10 dinosaurs are discovered by people who are not professionals, and many of them are found by kids. That's because we really don't have an idea where they are. We know a general region where dinosaurs lived, but the tricky thing is the land has to be the exact opposite of how it was millions of years ago. Fossils got preserved when dinosaurs died in a wet area and were covered by mud. So, you need an area that was wet then, but now is dry. Otherwise, they'll still be underwater."

TELL-TALE SIGNS OF FOSSILS

"Fossils have lots of tiny holes. That's where minerals got into the bone and made them very hard, like rocks. But remember, fossils aren't just bones. Eggs and footprints can get fossilized too. For bones, you want to not just look for little holes, but also pay attention to the shape. Bone fossils have rounded ends, or are curved like one of your ribs, but only much bigger."

DINO TEETH ARE A COMMON FIND

"You can find a lot of dinosaur teeth because when they were alive, dinosaurs would break off a lot of teeth when they were killing and eating other dinosaurs. They didn't care because another set of teeth would grow back in. Teeth fossils are pretty easy to recognize, meat eaters had serrated teeth where the edge kind of looks like a steak knife."

HOW TO REMOVE A FOSSIL

"If you find something you think is a fossil, you want to dig around a wide area to remove it from the ground or rock. Then you use tools like a toothbrush or screwdriver to gently remove the surrounding material. If you dig right into the bone, there's a good chance you'll break it."

ALWAYS LOOK DOWN

"A meat-eating dinosaur related to the Allosaurus was discovered on the coast of Portugal by a little girl. She was out walking around with her brother, who was a paleontologist, and had to go to the bathroom. She went behind something to get some privacy and she looked down and realized she was looking at dinosaur bones."

DINOSAURS HAD ACNE

"The first fossil I found was in Eastern Montana. I found a huge lump that was rounded on one end and had tiny holes in it. I brought it to an expert, and he said, 'Eh, that's a bony pimple from the head of a triceratops. We got a million of those. You can keep it.' So, it is sitting in my living room right now. I think it is very cool. To be the first person to touch something that was a living animal 65 million years ago? That's a great feeling."

PRACTICE DIGGING UP FOSSILS IN YOUR KITCHEN

Dino Don says a good way to practice gently removing a fossil is with a chocolate chip cookie. "Use a toothpick and see if you can remove a full chip without breaking the cookie." Or eating it.

VACATION BACK IN TIME

Here are some great places to see fossils in person.

- **Badlands National Park,** *South Dakota*
- **Big Bend National Park,** *Texas*
- **Dinosaur National Park,** *Colorado and Utah*
- **Grand Teton National Park,** *Wyoming*
- **Glacier National Park,** *Montana*

DID YOU KNOW?

The most complete skeleton of a T. Rex ever found is nicknamed "Sue," after the paleontologist Sue Hendrickson who found it.

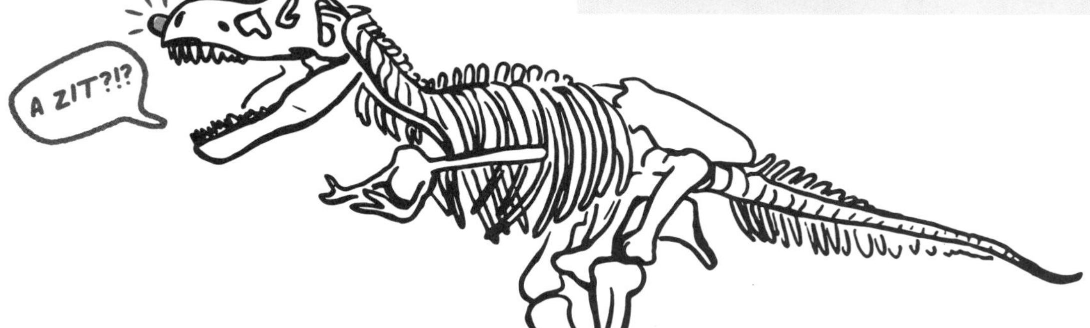

THE KING OF SCI-FI MONSTERS

Thankfully, Godzilla doesn't exist in real life. But if he did, here are some things his vet should know.

Since his first awakening, the radioactive, fire-spewing kaiju (a Japanese monster) has grown 200 feet and put on more than 150,000 tons. Godzilla is now 30 stories tall and weighs as much as a cruise ship. No actual animal could take the pressure of being so massive: It would overheat, its organs would implode, and it would need to mainline butter to get enough calories. For fun, we surveyed scientists to help us break down the beast's biology. If Godzilla were real, he would be an incredible specimen.

WEIGHT PROBLEMS

Given his height of 200 feet, Godzilla would weigh 164,000 tons. The heaviest creature to ever walk the earth in real life was the 100-ton dinosaur Argentinosaurus, which stood 70 feet tall, was 115 feet long, and had four limbs to distribute its enormous heft.

BAD TO THE BONE

The force on Godzilla's bones is roughly 20 times greater than the force on a T. Rex's, so his bones would need to be phenomenally strong—about twice as tough as some titanium alloys. Godzilla's cartilage would be about 12 times stronger than a human's, preventing his knees from exploding like overripe tomatoes—and making him the envy of basketball players everywhere.

THICK SKIN

Godzilla's exterior is tough. (Soldiers trying to kill him with puny rifles, really?) His crocodile-like hide would be embedded bony deposits that are like chain mail.

BAD BREATH

Godzilla is able to shoot atomic breath out of his mouth. So, if we were G's vet, we'd avoid telling them to open up and say "Aaaah."

DID YOU KNOW?

Paleontologist Kenneth Carpenter named a dinosaur he discovered after Godzilla, using his Japanese name Gojira. Carpenter says the Gojirasaurus was a meat eater that lived 210 million years ago.

HEART SIZE:
60 FEET ACROSS
100 TONS
ATOMIC BREATH
200 FT. TALL
BONES:
2x STRONGER THAN TITANIUM
CARTILAGE: 12x STRONGER THAN HUMANS
164,000 TONS

WHAT'S UP WITH AREA 51

For decades, conspiracy theorists say this secret military base in the Nevada desert has aliens behind its closed doors. Are they right?

ON EARLY MORNINGS, eagle-eyed visitors in the Las Vegas desert can spot strange lights in the sky moving up and down. No, it's not a UFO. It's actually the semisecret commuter airline using the call-sign "Janet" that transports workers from Las Vegas's McCarran Airport to Area 51, just north.

Since the base opened in the 1950s, "alien" aircraft have been reported. Though unlikely, the base's secretive history has invited conspiracies to run wild about what is truly concealed in the southern Nevada desert. But if not aliens, what is hiding behind the walls of Area 51?

When the Soviet Union lowered the Iron Curtain and attempted to block itself from contact with its allies and the Western world in the late 1940s, there was a near-total intelligence blackout to the rest of the world. Worried about the USSR's potential technology and intentions, President Eisenhower approved the secret development of a high-altitude spy plane called the U-2 in November 1954. The test site for the secret plane? The southern Nevada desert.

At the time, commercial airlines were flying at altitudes between 10,000 and 20,000 feet, compared to up to 38,000 feet today. Aircraft in the U-2 program could reach 60,000 feet. So, in 1944, seeing a plane at this seemingly unreachable height looked completely otherworldly to anyone below.

Commercial pilots started reporting the peculiarities right away. The base couldn't just announce that it was working on a spy plane, so "natural phenomena" or "high-altitude weather research" became the government's go-to explanations for the "UFO" sightings.

For decades, that answer worked. But then, in 1989, conspiracy theorist Bob Lazar went on Las Vegas local news and said that he'd seen aliens and had helped build alien spacecrafts while working at the base.

Without confirmation about what truly existed inside the base, wild speculation reigned for decades. Most theories pertained to galactic visitors tucked away somewhere, but other rumors were just as—if not more—sensational.

One of the more colorful rumors insists that the infamous 1947 Roswell crash was actually a Soviet aircraft piloted by mutated little people and the wreckage remains on the grounds of Area 51. Another is that the U.S. government filmed the 1969 moon landing in one of the base's hangars.

The CIA declassified parts of a report about the truth of the U-2 program that explained details of many of the early sightings by commercial pilots. But the lore of Area 51 remains strong.

Fact or fiction, people still gawk to see what lies beyond those chain link fences. And if anything is true about extraterrestrial beings, it's that they attract a lot of tourists.

In 1996, the state of Nevada renamed Route 375 — the highway closest to Area 51 — as the "Extraterrestrial Highway," and along the road visitors will also see places like the Alien Research Center and the Little A'Le'Inn. (Say it out loud to get it.)

While tourists are not permitted inside the base, it is legal to drive up to its front and back gates. Just remember, it is in the middle of the desert. So forget about E.T. wanting to phone home — E.T. wants a Gatorade and some sunscreen!

HOW TO TALK TO ALIENS

Douglas Vakoch, founder of Messaging Extraterrestrial Intelligence (METI), explains how his company is reaching out.

For decades we've listened for messages from intelligent life without success. "But what if other civilizations are also simply listening and not transmitting?" asks Vakoch, who founded METI in 2015 and is the former director of Interstellar Message Composition for the Search for Extraterrestrial Intelligence.

METI targets stars that are only 10 to 20 light-years away in hopes of establishing dialogue that can take place over mere decades, and not thousands of years. Using optical and radio transmitters, it sends pulses that convey basic math and physics. "We're likely to have those in common with extraterrestrials able to exchange radio signals," he says.

They've yet to make contact, but the recent increase in discoveries of potentially habitable exoplanets, such as the TRAPPIST-1 system, announced in February, gives METI 52 planets to focus on amid a galaxy of 100 billion options.

So, when are we going to hear back? "If we are incredibly lucky, we could potentially receive a reply within a lifetime," Vakoch says. More realistically, he admits, it could take thousands of years.

HOW TO SAFELY JUMP INTO A BLACK HOLE

WHOA!

What would it be like to visit—and even enter—a black hole? We asked the experts.

KNOW WHAT YOU'RE GETTING INTO

Black holes form when matter condenses into a tiny amount of space, like when a massive star collapses in on itself. This creates a point of infinitely strong gravity — a singularity — and a surrounding region that traps anything that gets too close, called the event horizon. Not even light can escape, which explains why it is called a black hole.

DON'T TURN INTO DINNER

Gravity is so intense that as you approach the event horizon you'd get stretched from head to toe in a process called spaghettification. (Yes, that means you'd get stretched out like a strand of spaghetti!)

BIGGER IS BETTER

To survive long enough to explore a black hole, you must find a big one, says Janna Levin, Ph.D., an astrophysicist at Barnard College of Columbia University. A supermassive black hole, like the one within M87, is over 3 million times wider than Earth. This gives you plenty of room to look around before you cross the event horizon—about 12 billion miles.

You would simply float across, and keep floating, for a while. In the biggest black holes, Levin says, "you might be able to make it for a year before you are ultimately demolished in the center."

LOOK OUT FOR THE RINGS!

Avoid black holes with accretion disks, which are fast-spinning rings of matter. They can heat up to millions of degrees and create "some of the largest magnetic fields that we've measured," says Leo Rodriguez, Ph.D., a theoretical physicist at Grinnell College in Iowa. Magnetic fields this strong would shut down your nervous system and stretch your atoms into skinny rods until you dissolve.

THE VIEW WILL BE AMAZING

If you purposely or accidentally cross the event horizon, you're in for a spectacular show. As you approach the black hole, you'll see the light of the universe warped by the black hole's intense gravity. "It will be like crossing into a funhouse mirror," Levin says. The light from stars will smear across the sky and you'll be given a window to the universe that contains eons of trapped light. "You would be able to see an entire history of the black hole since it was formed," Rodriguez says.

WANNA GO BACK HOME?

There is one potential exit, but you shouldn't count on it. Your black hole could double as a wormhole, which would transport you to another part of the universe. That sounds fun, unless you consider the fact that at that point, you would be pulled apart into your most basic particles. Ouch!

Make the Best Paper Airplane Ever

DIFFICULTY LEVEL

Barnaby Wainfan has worked on dozens of innovative aircraft. So, you can bet his paper airplane design is pretty good!

STUFF YOU'LL NEED

- **A sheet of paper**
- **Pen or pencil**
- **Scotch tape**
- **A paperclip**

1. Draw this airplane shape in the middle of a sheet of paper.

2. Fold the paper in half down the center of the plane. Cut along the perimeter to get a perfectly symmetrical aircraft.

3. Now fold: first, the wings, down along line No. 1. Then grab the tail in the center and fold it in the opposite direction along the same line, so it extends above the wings. Next, fold down along line No. 2.

4. At the seam where the wings meet, use a piece of Scotch tape to hold them together.

5. Add a standard paper clip beside the nose to balance the weight of the thinner nose with the plane's wide wings. Last, fold the flaps up along line No. 3.

6. After a test flight, troubleshoot by adjusting those folds. If the plane nosedives, bend the rear flaps to make them more vertical. If it swoops up and then dives straight down, flatten them.

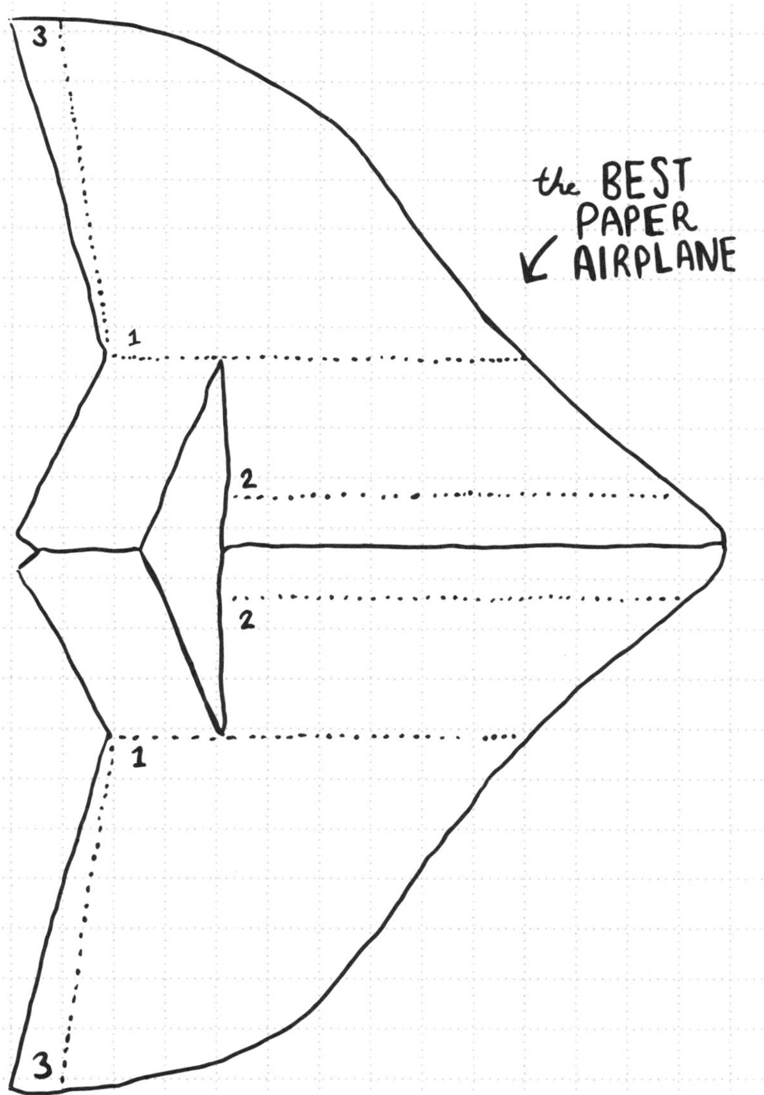
the BEST
PAPER
AIRPLANE
3
1
2
2
1
3

Sweet Science: How to Make Ice Cream With a Bag

DIFFICULTY LEVEL

EASY-PEASY

STUFF YOU'LL NEED

- **A resealable plastic bag**
- **1 cup half-and-half**
- **2 tablespoons granulated sugar**
- **½ teaspoon pure vanilla extract**
- **3 cups ice**
- **⅓ cup kosher salt**
- **Toppings of your choice**

1. In a small resealable plastic bag, combine half-and-half, sugar, and vanilla. Push out excess air and seal.

2. Into a large resealable plastic bag, combine ice and salt. Place a small bag inside the bigger bag and shake vigorously, seven to 10 minutes, until ice cream has hardened.

3. Remove from the bag and enjoy with your favorite ice cream toppings.

ICE CREAM FUN FACTS

TRY NOT TO GET BRAIN FREEZE AS YOU READ!

- The earliest version of ice cream was made in ancient China around 3,000 BC. It was crushed ice combined with fruit juices. No sprinkles?!
- Twelve gallons of milk are needed to make just one gallon of ice cream. Thanks, cows!
- The third Sunday of July is National Ice Cream Day. How will you celebrate?

INDEX

NOTE: Page numbers in *italics* indicate projects.

DECODER KEY

A	×	**G**	→	**M**	●	**S**	☽	**Y**	☒
B	◆	**H**					**N**	○	**T**	◊	**Z**	‖
C	❙	**I**	△	**O**	☺	**U**	▲		
D	★	**J**	^	**P**	⊙	**V**	⊗		
E	✳	**K**	≈	**Q**	✓	**W**	▣		
F	■	**L**	□	**R**	✚	**X**	⊘		

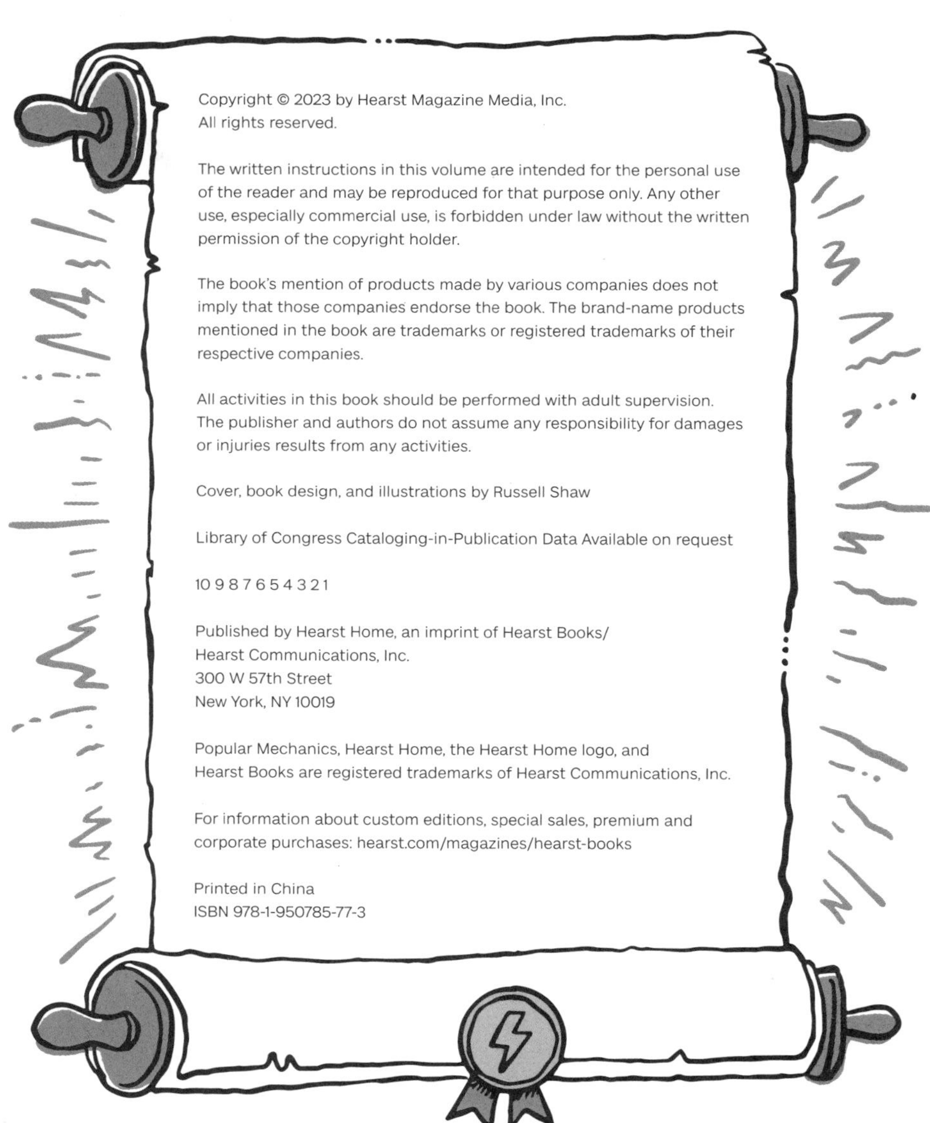

Cover, book design, and illustrations by Russell Shaw

Library of Congress Cataloging-in-Publication Data Available on request

10 9 8 7 6 5 4 3 2 1

Published by Hearst Home, an imprint of Hearst Books/
Hearst Communications, Inc.
300 W 57th Street
New York, NY 10019

For information about custom editions, special sales, premium and corporate purchases: hearst.com/magazines/hearst-books

Printed in China
ISBN 978-1-950785-77-3